I AM

The God Who Leads

By

Valerie Henderson

I AM

The God Who Leads

By

Valerie Henderson

PO Box 2132

Keller, Texas 76244

USA

I AM

The God Who Leads

ISBN 13 TP: 978-1-962808-18-7

ISBN 13 eBook: 978-1-962808-19-4

Cover Design by Darian Horner Design
(www.darianhorner.com)
Image: stock.adobe.com #292566765

First Edition: May 2025

10 9 8 7 6 5 4 3 2 1 0

Printed in the United States of America

Table of Contents

Acknowledgements

In loving memory of John, my beloved husband, whose support and encouragement were instrumental in the early stages of this book. Though he passed away before its completion, he really liked the idea of it and wanted to see it completed.

I extend my heartfelt gratitude to Jim R. and Wa S. for graciously listening as I read each chapter aloud to them during the writing process—their feedback and encouragement meant the world to me.

A sincere thank you to Pastor Robin Gates for contributing the Foreword, to Wendy Selvig for her thoughtful editing, and to Darian Horner for her creative and inspiring cover artwork.

Foreword

America is being enveloped by a growing spiritual darkness that seems to be affecting virtually every area of our culture-including much of the church in the Western world. There is little doubt that there is a need for spiritual renewal in this nation and beyond, a need for insights into leadership from our God who leads, and what can be gleaned from the scriptures that teach us His leadership for our lives.

In this compilation of vignettes presented by my friend Valerie Henderson, she has masterfully revealed to us just how our God leads us. Through the stories of the likes of Jonah, Nehemiah, Jeremiah, Moses, Ezekiel, Noah, Abraham, Isaac, Joshua and others, Valerie weaves a picture of God's leadership style in teaching us to follow Him. Regardless of whether you have been a casual or ardent student of the Bible, you will have new revelations of understanding, that may bring tears to your eyes or eureka moments that will enrich your spiritual walk! Probably both! Either way, it is a win-win for the Kingdom.

I first met Valerie at a men's shelter where I was the Administrator and Pastor. She asked to teach a Bible class to the men. I made room for her in the schedule. I was cautious to allow a woman to teach at a men's shelter but was encouraged by the Holy Spirit to give her an opportunity. Both the men and I were blessed. Her class became a favorite with the men, and on the evenings that she would teach, there would always be two or three men who would walk Valerie to her car asking questions.

You won't be able to walk her to her car, but you will be blessed to walk with her through the insights and revelations in this book. And remember, a humble, committed, passionate servant of God is a perfect conduit for God to release His unparalleled power.

Robin Gates

Ascent7 Ministries,

An Isaiah 58:6-7 Ministry

"Wherever the Lord Leads"

Preface

This book is filled with 30 short stories, divided into three volumes with 10 chapters in each. The title of the book, *I AM: The God Who Leads* sets the pace for what is written on its pages. It is an incredible spiritual adventure and journey that will send the reader's thoughts into a curious hunger to know more about the subject. It gives a new, fresh look at God's wondrous leadership through each volume.

The short stories are designed to be spiritually thought-provoking, in which will challenge the reader to experience God's divine leadership from His view. God explains His leadership throughout scripture, and with His Word, we can learn about the different styles He chooses to wisely lead us.

May each person who reads this book gain wisdom, with knowledge and understanding of just how important it is to allow God's leadership to influence our style of leadership. God's leadership can help us be better leaders in our families, our churches, in the workplace and in the communities, we live in.

My hope is that the reader will gain fresh new insight and hunger to learn more about God's intentional superb leadership that can give us favor before kings and nations. And may you enjoy reading this book as much as I enjoyed writing it.

Shalom,

Valerie Henderson

Volume 1

Weather Phenomenal Leadership

Chapter 1

Weather Leadership

Recently, God revealed an interesting clue to His style of leadership that represents Him best. I was surprised to find out how He has used weather leadership to guide men throughout history. I will explain as I unfold the story that led up to the subject.

A friend asked me to read Deuteronomy 32:1-4 and reflect on what the Lord might reveal regarding a comment I had made about experiencing headaches due to barometric pressure. Sometimes I get headaches when the pressure changes. So, I accepted the challenge and for two days I prayed and sought God's guidance. During that time, I waited for Him to speak, hoping He would offer wisdom about the connection between my headaches and the shifting barometric pressure. Through this process, I learned that when God speaks, it's always with purpose. He desires us to listen carefully because He is about to share something important that will strengthen our faith and deepen our relationship with Him.

Let us move ahead here and read in Deuteronomy:

Give hear, O heavens, and I will speak; and hear, O earth, the words of mouth. Let my teaching drop as the rain, my speech distill as the dew, as raindrops on the tender herb, and the showers on the grass. For I proclaim the name of the Lord: ascribe greatness to our God, He is the Rock, His work is perfect; for all His ways are justice, a God of truth and without injustice; righteous and upright is He (Deuteronomy 32:1-4).

Using the side note of scriptures beside those verses in Deuteronomy, the Lord led me to Isaiah 55:

For as the rain comes down, and the snow from heaven and do not return there. But water the earth. And make it bring forth and bud, that it may give seed to the sower and bread to the eater. So shall My word be that goes forth from My mouth, it shall not return to Me void. But it shall accomplish what I please. And it shall prosper in the thing for which I sent it. (Isaiah 55:10-11)

After pondering on these scriptures, I then asked the Lord if that was it. I picked up my Bible and shifted it to a better position in my lap and I lost grip of it. It fell out of my hands and when it landed back in my lap, it fell open to 2 Samuel 23. I looked and saw the subtitle and it read, "David's Last Words." I then proceeded to read verses 1-4, which reads,

> *¹ Now these are the last words of David. Thus says David the son of Jesse; thus say the man raised up on high. The anointed of the God of Jacob, and the sweet psalmist of Israel: ² 'The Spirit of the Lord spoke by me, and His word was on my tongue. ³ The God of Israel said the Rock of Israel spoke to me: he who rules over men must be just, ruling in the fear of God. ⁴ And he shall be like the light of the morning when the sun rises, a morning without clouds, like the tender grass springing out of the earth; by clear shining after rain.'*

All of a sudden, I saw an incredible new twist of information on weather leadership the Lord was mixing into the study. It wasn't just about His spoken Word; He wanted to move me into the surprise element of weather and how He uses it to speak and lead. So now let's compare the information from all three chapters and see what the Lord is teaching us about His style of leadership.

First, He tells us of His Word to hear it and then lets its teaching drop like rain, and lets His speech be as the dew, as raindrops on a tender herb that showers the grass. We must proclaim the name of the Lord for our life and lift up His greatness, for He is our rock, our stability, His work is perfect, and all His ways are justice; He is truth and without injustice, He is righteous and is upright always. If we give ear to the Lord when

He speaks, it will rain down on us and water our spirit and soul so that we can produce fruit for the kingdom of God. God says that when He releases His Word from His mouth, it shall go forth and not return to Him void. But it shall accomplish what He pleases, and it will prosper in the thing for which He sent it to do.

Now let's add David's last words to the mix. It says the Spirit of the Lord spoke to him and God's Word was on his tongue. David mentions Him as the God of Israel and the Rock of Israel and then says He who rules over men must be just, ruling in the fear of God. And He shall be like the light of the morning when the sun rises, a morning without clouds, like the tender grass springing out of the earth, by clear shining after a rain.

Can you see now how the Spirit of the Lord is speaking about His style of leadership? This is the example we should follow whenever we lead over men. It is really inspirational how God uses the weather to explain how to lead others. It is powerful because none of it could come to pass if He had not spoken His Word first. When He speaks all of Heaven and Earth listen because He is truth and a just God and leads like a fresh spring morning with no clouds in the sky.

Another example of weather leadership we can see from these verses is God's character and the traits He possesses to lead all creation. When the Israelites were in the desert for forty years, God led them by day with a cloud; giving them shade from the sun, keeping them cool during the day, and letting their enemy know God was still on patrol watching over His people. At night, He gave them fire that gave them light in the darkness of the desert, it gave them warmth when the desert was cold and once again it gave a visual to their enemy that God was still on duty watching over His people.

Can you see the pattern God is cutting out for us by using weather phenomena to lead and guide us? He used His best leadership skills and traits to keep the Israelites safe and sound while they lived in the desert. By doing so, God is reminding us that He does not change; He is the same God in the day and at night. That is why He is the same yesterday, today and forever. That is why the enemy of God does not like Him, because He is steadfast, He does not change and there is no buying God off to look the other way. God holds fast in all things; He is true and stands strong in His justice. God is our leader, He is our Father and the One who is a rock, steadfast in all He speaks and does.

The wisdom from all three verses is that whatever we speak from our mouth we must be careful because our words will not come back to us void. That is why God's Word says, there is life and death in the tongue. We cannot always see what is in the air around us, but we can know that God is there watching, leading and guiding us with His forever steadfast weather leadership no matter what the weather is in our physical or spiritual atmosphere. Let us be reminded God is not a fair-weather leader and neither should we be.

Lord, let me follow in your footsteps of greatness, a leader that leads like a beautiful spring morning with the sun shining with clear skies. Amen.

Chapter 2

God Sets the Pace

Leading has always been an important trait that our heavenly Father has possessed since the beginning of time. God sets the pace for all of mankind because that is what a Father is supposed to do for His children. It is important to understand God's style of leadership so we can mirror it as we grow and mature in our relationship with Him. God wants us to know how to properly lead one another so we can be righteous leaders in every phase of our lives.

It's interesting how God has used the weather over and over throughout scripture to teach us about His style of leadership. When the Lord came down on Mount Sinai to meet with the children of Israel, there was lightning, thunder and clouds. I admire how He used the weather to get the Israelites' attention; it gave value to His authority. It let the people know that He was serious about being their God who brought them out of Egypt and saved them from Pharaoh's army who pursued them across the Red Sea.

Later, Moses was commissioned to build a temple for God to dwell in while He led the Israelites through the desert. The temple was a portable tent, so when the Lord was ready for them to move to a new location, they could take the temple with them while they journeyed to the promised land. What is interesting is that the first time the temple was erected and ready for God's presence to arrive, it did so in full force. His glory cloud changed the atmosphere of the temple; it gave a visual of God's approval so the Israelites could see He was pleased with their obedience for following His instructions for creating the temple.

It is fascinating what appeared over the tent of the Tabernacle on the first day; God set the pace for worship quickly when His glory showed up in the form of a cloud. The glory cloud was so heavy that not even Moses could enter the Holy of Holies. Once again, God used a simple weather phenomenon to express His leadership. It's amazing because a cloud is made of dust and moisture, just as man is, so it makes sense why God would use a cloud to fill His glory with, representing both Himself and man because we are created in His image.

God cared above and beyond for the children of Israel. His glory sustained the Israelites during their time in the desert; they never went hungry or thirsty, and their clothes, shoes and bodies did not wear out while he led them to the promised land of milk and honey.

Ezekiel 37 is a good reminder of what happens to a people when they lose their faith and are living far away from God, such as the Israelites were. The Lord told Ezekiel to prophesy to the valley of dry bones. The Lord said,

> 'Prophesy to these bones, and say to them, "O dry bones, hear the word of the Lord! Thus says the Lord God to these bones; 'Surely I will cause breath to enter into you, and you shall live. I will put sinews on you and bring flesh upon you, cover you with skin and put breath in you, and you shall live. Then you shall know that I am the Lord.'"' (Ezekiel 37:4-7)"

Though the prophet Ezekiel spoke this prophecy long after Moses, it is still a painted picture of what took place in the days of Moses because God took them while they were in captivity, spiritually dead and dry because they had forgotten His statues while they lived in Egypt in slavery. As God leads them through the desert, He breathes life into them and sustains them for 40 years. Let's finish reading what happened to the dry bones in Ezekiel. It says in verses 9-11:

> [9] ... 'Prophesy to the breath, prophesy, son of man, and say to the breath, "Thus says the Lord God: 'Come from the four winds, O breath, and breathe on these slain, that they may live.'"' [10] So I prophesied as He commanded me, and

the breath came into them, and they lived and stood upon their feet, an exceedingly great army. ¹¹ Then He said to me, 'Son of man, these bones are the whole house of Israel. They indeed say, 'Our bones are dry, our hope is lost, and we ourselves are cut off!''

(Can you hear the voices of the Israelites in the desert saying something similar and complaining about how they wanted to go back to Egypt instead of forward because of the challenges of the desert?) Have you ever found yourself saying something likewise in your own life? There is no doubt that most people have, so you don't have to be too hard on yourself; there is still hope for us all. Let's read just a little bit more about Ezekiel's mission with the dry bones.

God said to Ezekiel,

¹² *'Therefore prophesy and say to them, "Thus says the Lord God: 'Behold, O My people, I will open your graves and cause you to come up from your graves and bring you into the land of Israel. ¹³ Then you shall know that I am the Lord, when I have opened your graves, O My people, and brought you up from the graves. ¹⁴ I will put My Spirit in you, and you shall live, and I will place you in your own land. Then you shall know that I, the Lord, have spoken it and performed it, says the Lord'"' (Ezekiel 37:12-14).*

As we have just read, what a great similarity it is that death passed over the Israelite's doors, and they did not die.

Ezekiel's prophecy was not just for the Israelites; it remains a timeless message for all generations, offering hope to those trapped in spiritual bondage. It reveals God's power to restore life and empower people to step into His kingdom living. When the heart of man is living in sin, his soul and spirit are in captivity, far away from God. Then our spirit man must be given true life from the Lord by letting God breathe life into it, changing the atmosphere of the heart, so He can call the four winds of His breath into our flesh, soul and spirit to live so that death will pass over us. Jesus' resurrection creates a great picture of being raised from the dead with God's breath and glory. I can only imagine how strong both were when the power combined raised Jesus from the grave. When we allow God to live in our earthly body, we are making our body a living temple for Him to reside in and a mobile temple that enables Him to lead and sustain us like the Israelites were. His living Word in us will not come back to Him void. He wants to give us His breath of life so we will live and not die. Then we will receive His Holy Spirit, the glory cloud, and by doing so, we will experience the power of both like Jesus did, so we will know Him now and not later.

God sets the pace with His weather leadership, and all we have to do is absorb it into every aspect of our lives and by doing so, it will guide us into uncharted territory with God, activating growth in our faith in Him. Our comforter, the Holy Spirit, will be at the forefront and will encompass us every step of the way into a new horizon with the Lord. Hebrews 4:12-13 says,

11

¹² For the Word of God is living and powerful, and sharper than any two-edged sword, piercing even to the division of the soul and spirit, and of joints and marrow, and is a discerner of the thoughts and intents of the heart. ¹³ And there is no creature hidden from His sight, but all things are naked and open to the eyes of Him to whom we must give account.

May God activate His Word that commands the breath of life to come from the four winds, that awakens our soul and spirit like never before, and then He will fill our souls that thirst for Him as a deer pants for water, filling it with His living water as distill dew that creates a Holy moisture from His Spirit the cloud of glory, and all the while, engaging our soul's direction towards His loving care that will come down from Heaven like the beauties of holiness, from the womb of the morning. Amen.

Chapter 3

A Hand That Writes

It was a Tuesday morning, and I drove my husband, John, across town to a business meeting. I waited in the car while he went into his meeting because we had to go to a friend's house to do a painting estimate afterward. While I waited in the car, I read my Bible, seeking the Lord on what I was to write about in this chapter on His leadership. I became very sleepy, so I put down my Bible in the passenger seat, reclined my chair and fell asleep; and had a dream. I saw a heavenly hand appear, holding a pen in a writing position. I immediately said to myself in the dream, "A hand that writes, just like in the Bible." I soon woke up after the dream and was astonished by the dream. I did not see what the hand was writing. However, it did not matter because the Lord was telling me His hand would be guiding my hand while I wrote this chapter and that the hand pertained to what I was about to write. I love it! I can now move forward at an even greater confidence and pace that I am on the right track sharing with others about God's impeccable leadership throughout the ages.

The dream helps me to zero in on my search in Genesis to learn more about God's leadership through the story of how He created the earth, man and all of creation. It reveals that His wisdom is far above what any man can imagine. The beauty of the story is breathtaking and is filled with the mystery of how God makes decisions that become reality. The story of creation gives hope for all because we can have joy in knowing our heavenly Father is teaching us about the infinity of His leadership through all the splendor of His creation. We can know we serve an eternal God who is not flesh, but He is Spirit.

Genesis 1:1-2 says:

¹ In the beginning, God created the heavens and the earth.
² The earth was without form, and void; and darkness was on the face of the deep. And the Spirit of God was hovering over the face of the waters.

Wow! God's Spirit was hovering over the face of the waters, commanding them to wake up so it could help sustain life on planet Earth for all ages to come. God is an infinite creator who is leading all His creation into a future that would be bright regardless of its disobedience to Him that was going to evolve; we can gather through His creation teaching that He loves mankind and wants to give us faith to do the impossible. He gave Noah the faith to build the ark and prepare for rainfall from the heavens, which he had never seen or even knew of before God told him of it, which is interesting since Noah had already been alive 600 years at that very moment in time. Noah was born at such a time in history to help save mankind from extinction off the face of the earth. Thank God for Noah's righteousness. He stood in the gap for us all. A funny note here is that it proves you're never too old to obey the Lord and carry out what He has commanded you to do. On a more serious note, God does not set boundaries when it comes to age and ministry. He chooses whom He chooses, whether young or old, as history has proved it throughout time.

Another great subject that Genesis teaches us about is righteous leadership; it is a gift from our Creator because not all men possess such an ability. God chose Noah because he was the only just man and perfect in his generation alive on planet Earth. He was like a messiah in his time; He called out to man to repent of his sins for 120 years, and then God used a wooden boat to save mankind so He could bring redemption to us all.

Noah loved God, and therefore, He was chosen, he and his family to be saved from a massive worldwide flood that would destroy mankind and every living thing off the face of the earth, except for the living animals and so forth that were to be put in the ark with Noah and his family. All this happened because of man's sin, and God was sorry He had made man.

As we learn from reading Genesis, there were actually two types of floods. We learn the first flood was about the flood of sins mankind was swimming in; they had chosen a life raft of disobedience that would soon sink with them on it. They would lose their life by the very waters that God had hovered over at the beginning of creation to help sustain them on planet Earth. The waters of Heaven and Earth would have to take the breath of life from those left behind and destroy them off the face of the earth.

I can only imagine God's broken heart to have to destroy His creation with a massive flood and then to make the decision to start over with a better plan for mankind. This leads us back to the hand I saw in the dream; the Lord revealed later that evening the full purpose of the hand appearing to me was more about God rewriting man's future with the flood. The reason is that man keeps falling into the disobedience of sin, and when he does, it usually causes a shift in the spiritual realm of man's relationship with His Creator, God the Father. The shifting in change is not created by the Father but by man continually rejecting God. We have to remember God does not change; He is the same yesterday, today and forever. It is pretty amazing how God is slow to anger, but when His patience is finally run out, man has to pay up for his sin.

The beautiful result of the flood is the rainbow. It reminds us that God made an everlasting covenant between Him, Noah and all creation on Earth, never to flood the earth again. Powerful indeed, the God of all leading mankind into a bright future, using weather phenomena such as a rainbow, bursting it with living stripes of color so that it will give us a visual of His covenant above our heads in the sky with the clouds. I always wondered why God gave rainbow strips of colors, and now we know they were put there for the future for mankind's salvation, so it would be a reminder: by His stripes, we are healed because Jesus was wounded for our transgressions. Amen.

Chapter 4

Get Out of Your Country

Now, the Lord said to Abram, "Get out of your country." Do you ever struggle to follow God's calling because you feel stuck in a rut? Maybe you're living near family, enjoying a quiet and comfortable life, thinking, *I'm doing okay. Everything is good. I'll just stay here forever.*

Then, suddenly, God knocks on the door of your heart, calling you in a new direction—one that takes you far from friends and family. As the reality sets in, your mind fills with *what-ifs,* your hands grow clammy, and excuses pile up, convincing you that you can't do what God is asking.

The problem with not doing what the Lord has asked you to do is that your disobedience becomes a sin and soon fears, and then disobedience takes control instead of trusting the Lord. In the words of Franklin D. Roosevelt, the famous U.S. president, *'The only thing we have to fear is fear itself.'* Overcoming fear is our power to excel in God's promises for us.

Even after the flood, believe it or not, man sunk back into sin and continued not to listen to the Lord. However, God did find a few people who still wanted to follow Him. God chose Abram being one of those people and one day the Lord appeared to him and said,

> *Get out of your country, from your family and from your father's house, to a land that I will show you. I will make you a great nation; I will bless you and make your name great; and you shall be a blessing. I will bless those who bless you, and I will curse him who curses you, and in you, all the families of the earth shall be blessed. (Genesis 12:1-3)*

Genesis 12 through 13 tells us that Abram packed up his household and left with his nephew Lot and his entire household, and they journeyed near Egypt. Abram told his wife Sarah to tell the Egyptians she was his sister, for he feared they would kill him and take her because of her countenance of beauty. Long story short, she did, and Pharaoh showed favor to Abram and gave him camels, sheep, oxen, male and female servants, female donkeys and other things such as gold and silver. But the Lord plagued Pharaoh and his house with great plagues because of Sarah, Abram's wife.

¹⁸ And Pharaoh called Abram and said, "What is this you have done to me? Why did you not tell me that she was your wife? ¹⁹ Why did you say she was your sister"? I might have taken her as my wife. Now, therefore, here is your wife; take her and go your way. (Genesis 12:18-19)

So, Pharaoh commanded his men concerning him, and they sent him away, with his wife and all that he had.

By the time Abram left Egypt he had gained more riches and had become a very wealthy man. Unfortunately, there was a division between the herders of Abram and Lots, so Abram decided to split from his nephew Lot to keep the peace between them because they were brethren, and so he gave Lot the first choice of which direction he wanted to go. Lot chose land near Sodom because of the lush green pastures and plenty of water. So, Abram took his family and went to Canaan.

After Abram separated from Lot, the Lord said to Abram:

Lift your eyes now and look from the place where you are—northward, southward, eastward and westward: for all the land which you see I give you and your descendants forever. And I will make your descendants as the dust of the earth; so that if a man could number the dust of the earth, then your descendants also could be numbered. (Genesis 13:14)

Later, we learn that Abram fought in a war with the ungodly king of Sodom and won. He did not take any booty because he did not want the king of Sodom to say he had made Abram rich. Abram only wanted the Lord's approval. Because he wanted it to be said that he trusted in the Lord, who sustained him and blessed him with riches. Abram truly trusted in the Lord, and afterward the war with Sodom's king, the Word of the Lord came to Abram in a vision, saying, "Do not be afraid, Abram. I am your shield, your exceedingly great reward." What God is teaching us through Abrams's story is to trust His leadership beyond what our physical man knows; that faith without works is dead. When we move ahead in faith and trust God, who knows best for us, it then will help us to gain riches beyond this earth, which is God Himself. Our trust in God permits to take over as the CEO of our fears, which means we can cross eternally over to gain heavenly treasures; it puts us in a position where we can be given the desires of our hearts because we first trusted Him. It allows Him to take care of us with His impeccable, fearless leadership, catapulting us into His infinity of blessings forever.

Though Abram attained an exceeding number of blessings, he told God he was lacking the blessing of a male child that was directly from Sarah. God had compassion and told Abram to step outside and look upward toward the night sky. The Lord said:

'Look towards the heaven, and count the stars if you are able to number them.' And He said to him, 'So shall your descendants be.' (Genesis 15:5)

The plan combining the two blessings from the dust to the stars, God now was leaving no space in between Earth and Heaven without a blessing by Him. Even so, Abraham falls on the ground laughing in his heart because he is 99 years old and Sarah is 90. Regardless, God kept His promise by the next year, their son Isaac was born. I am sure there was a different kind of laughter in their home after Sarah gave birth to Isaac. By the time Isaac was born, Sarah and Abraham were already using the new names the Lord had given them. This is another interesting factor because that meant God was elevating them to a whole new level of faith; a name change on the door of their faith meant God was upgrading their benefits to CEO level because now they were ready to cross eternally over and He was managing their future to establish a covenant with Isaac that would be everlasting and to all his descendants after him.

The Lord also had Abraham circumcise himself and all the men of his household. God's plan was to set apart Abraham and his household from all other families on the earth that did not serve God but rejected Him.

God's blessing was with Abraham and Sarah, who are the mother and father of all nations that love God and serve Him. And now we are to circumcise our hearts, setting ourselves apart from God. The blessings of Abraham, Sarah and Isaac are our inheritance, and therefore, we should cling to the covenant the Lord promised to us through them.

God kept our eternal future intact through Abraham's son, Isaac. Now God uses His son Jesus to increase Abraham's descendants into redemption through Jesus being our exceeding reward now and forever. God is our ultimate reward and desires to lead us into a bright future, branding the initials CEO on the door of our faith so now we can let Christ Erase the Obscurity of disbelief from our hearts. Therefore, we will be able to cross eternally over to God our Father.

In Mark, Jesus told the rich man who was trying to gain salvation through his earthly riches, He said to him:

> *One thing you lack: Go your way, sell whatever you have and give to the poor, and you will have treasure in heaven; and come, take up your cross, and follow me. (Mark 10:21)*

We, as believers, must be ready at all times to have our faith intact so we can be ready to get out of our country if God so calls us to. Therefore, deny yourself take up His cross daily, and follow Him. Amen.

Chapter 5

Before I Formed You

While Lot and Abram were still traveling together as a team, their herdsmen were having petty rivalries with each other because of jealousy and such. Finally, Abram was finished with all the arguing between the men and decided it was time to split ways with Lot and his household. Abram thought it through and decided the best way to handle parting ways with Lot, his brethren, would be to give him the first choice of which direction He wanted to take.

Abram said to Lot," If you go left, I will go right or vice versa." Abram did this to keep the peace between them, and Lot decided to go east towards Sodom because he saw the Jordan River and the beautiful pastures and decided selfishly that was the best land and place to take his family. He only considered his selfish desires and not his family or Abram.

Lot went towards Sodom, which was a very sinful place to live in or about. Lot did not give any thought that his family or others in his household might not be spiritually strong enough to live in such a sinful, out-of-control place that rejected God and His commandments. Lot put his whole household in jeopardy, and eventually, it would cause him to lose his entire family and fortune.

Petty rivalries can cloud one's judgment, causing strife and envy. It is important for believers in Christ to pull together even when there is a disagreement amongst themselves. Satan loves to conquer and divide. When unity breaks apart a family, friendship or ministry of any sort, there will always be someone to suffer with greater consequences because it can lead to bitterness, backsliding and so forth. Let's search a little deeper on what happened to Lot and his family. Later, there would be a rebellion in four cities, and one of those cities was Sodom, where lots resided. Eventually, Lot and all his family and wealth were taken captive by the king, who defeated Sodom. One of Lot's men's servants escaped and fled back to Abram and told him about Lot being taken. It was incredible; Abram responded quickly; he armed his 318 trained men, and they went to battle against five kings and their armies. With God's help, Abram defeated them, and he was able to bring back Lot, all his goods and women, children and other people.

What is amazing even though Lot had chosen unwisely, it did not stop Abram from rescuing his nephew from the hands of the enemy; this story is so similar to the story of a shepherd having 100 sheep, and if one comes up missing, the shepherd will go into search and rescue mode to find that one lost sheep leaving the 99 to bring the one lost back home safely. Abram had learned from God's superb leadership that fear was not a factor to stop him from helping his own kin out of a dangerous situation, even if it meant going into harm's way to help.

God honored Abram for the battle won, and then Melchizedek, king of Salem, brought out bread and wine; he was the priest of God Most High. And he blessed him and said: "Blessed be Abram of God Most High, Possessor of Heaven and Earth; and blessed be God Most High, who has delivered the enemies into your hand." And Abram then gave him a tithe and did not take any booty from the war. God was paying attention and blessed Abram for his righteous judgment and generosity with the king of Salem.

Melchizedek means "king of righteousness," and Salem means "king of peace." Which is a perfect picture of Christ? God was purposely mirroring the future for redemption for all the people of the earth. Nothing was a coincidence that was happening in Lot and Abram's lives. God was setting up salvation for all mankind. The decisions each man made in his own personal life set in motion consequences that would carry on long after they were gone from this earth. God is never fooled when a man makes his own decisions without involving Him in them. We soon learn this is what Lot did. He went back to Sodom with his family, and God sent two angels to destroy it along with the city of Gomorrah.

When the angels arrived, they were going to spend the night out in the open gathering place of the city of Sodom, but Lot persuaded them to come into his home for the night because he knew the men of the city wanted to lie with them. After the men went into Lot's house, the men of the city tried to get into the house to get the men's angels, and Lot tried to stop the men from wanting the angels, but they would not listen to him. The angels ended up striking those men blind that were near the door trying to get into Lot's house; so, they could not find the door to open it. Sodom and Gomorrah had become so tragically filled with acts of sin of every kind that God's patience had run out for both places. The lesson we are learning here is that Lot had become so complacent about the sin in his environment that nobody would listen to him, which rendered him useless in that dire situation.

Soon, the angels would have to lead Lot, his wife and two daughters out of the city of Sodom to safety so they could destroy Sodom and Gomorrah. They were instructed not to look back, but Lot's wife did and turned into a pillar of salt. Her disobedience caused her to perish along with the people of both cities. Fire and brimstone rained down on the two cities like a great furnace, and smoke rose in the sky. God showed compassion to Lot and his daughters because of Abrams's righteousness, who stood in the gap for his nephew and family. The power of prayer can save many generations, and we may never see the results, but God will, and that is all that matters. Lot's comfort with sin had overflowed to his wife, and unfortunately, she perished because of it. God says we cannot serve two masters; we will either love one or hate the other. The lesson we are learning here is that the effect of the petty rivalry that divided Lot from his uncle's leadership would come back on him with dire consequences.

God destroying Sodom and Gomorrah with fire and brimstone from Heaven is another prime example of His weather leadership, which speaks volumes of how God feels about man committing sin and rejecting righteousness. His patience had run out, and now he would be setting in motion the future of how he would deal with man's sin if no repentance were foreseen.

How do we set up our future to be protected under the promises of Abram and Isaac? It is pretty simple: we must turn away from self-driven ambitions that do not line up with the righteousness of God. The decisions we make in our lives can have a domino effect on all present and future generations. Abraham's decision to live under the protection of God represented a foreshadowing of the future that had to happen so that redemption from God's Son, the king of peace and righteousness, would usher in salvation for mankind.

In 1 Peter 4:17-18, it says:

17 For the time has come for judgment to begin at the house of God; and if it begins with us first, what will be

29

the end of those who do not obey the gospel of God?
[18] Now, If the righteous one is scarcely saved, where will the ungodly and the sinner appear?

Chapter 6

God's Stock

It was amazing; it was a Monday evening on a November night, and I had been thinking about this chapter and what the Lord would have me write within its pages. I have been praying for an answer for about three weeks. Well, tonight is that night, and I am very intrigued by what the Lord told me while I brushed my teeth. I could not help but laugh out loud about it because my mouth was foaming over with toothpaste, and God spoke the words, "God's stock." It made me laugh because God has such a great sense of humor. I know He did it because He knows I love it when He is spontaneous. I always include the Father in my daily routine of getting ready for my day or even while prepping for bedtime. So, it does not really surprise me that He chose to tell me what He wanted to talk about in this chapter while I brushed my teeth. He shared with me that His leadership is about taking stock and creating stock, but not the way man does. God's stock is in people, not material things. That's what Jesus said, to follow Him, and He will make us fishers of men.

God is not against a person creating wealth, most assuredly. However, that is not the point He is making here. God likes investing His time into creating relationships with His creation because He knows if He does, it will yield a much greater return on His investments in men. Our Father in Heaven is very wealthy and owns cattle on a thousand hills. He wants to encourage us to think about investing our resources into humans because money itself has no real value except if a human chooses to pick it up and spend it on something they consider of value to them. God considers man to be a great value, or He most certainly would not have allowed His only Son to die on the cross for the redemption of man's sin.

God took stock in Abraham and Sarah, and they were given Isaac, and he went on to succeed his father in receiving the blessing that God had promised Abraham. God picked Rebekah to be Isaac's wife. She was barren like Sarah was, however, I believe that was in God's plan all along because He was able to show them it was Him who would bring about every blessing He had promised to Abraham, giving him future generations that he would never meet. God not only opened Rebekah's womb to have a child, but He gave her twin sons, who would become two nations.

God does take stock in people, and through Abraham's story, that is very evident. Though there are many stories in the Bible that reveal it as well, we can ultimately see how God wants us to observe His leadership in a new perspective in how well He will invest His energy, time and love into mankind to bring about the promise He made to sustain Abraham's future generations for many ages to come.

So, when God calls you to do something, do it quickly and with a heart of gladness knowing He will provide for you to accomplish the mission He has set before you. Now, let's observe what He did for Isaac. In Genesis 26, it says there was a famine in the land; Isaac went to Abimelech, King of Philistines', in Gerar.

> *2 Then the Lord appeared to him and said: 'Do not go down to Egypt; live in the land of which I shall tell you. 3 Dwell in this land, and I will be with you and bless you; for to you and your descendants I give all these lands, and I will perform the oath which I swore to Abraham, your father. 4 And I will make your descendants multiply as the stars of heaven; I will give to your descendants all these lands; and in your seed, all the nations of the earth shall be blessed; 5 because Abraham obeyed My voice and kept My charge, My commandments, My statutes, and My laws'. (Genesis 26:2-5)*

I personally can see another 'wow' moment for believers all over the world through Abraham and Isaac's story. We must take a stance against the negative in our lives, step up to the plate of righteousness, and step into the promises that God had already set in place for us even before we were born. We must follow in the footsteps of our blessed forefathers, and then we will be blessed. God ended up blessing Isaac beyond what he could ever imagine.

Isaac stayed in Gerar; it's almost comical because Isaac did the same as his father did with Sarah. Isaac told King Abimelech that Rebekah was his sister; I can see how God was serious about giving both him and his dad knock-out gorgeous wives, that they had to say their wives were their sisters to prevent themselves from being killed, so the wives would not be stolen from them. The king soon discovered that Rebekah was Isaac's wife. As a result, He blessed them with protection, ordered everyone to leave them alone, and warned that anyone who harmed them would face the death penalty.

We can go on to read that Isaac sowed in the land and reaped in the same year a hundredfold, and the Lord blessed him. The man began to prosper and continued prospering until he became very prosperous, for he had possessions of flocks and possessions of herds and a great number of servants. Isaac had become so wealthy that even the Philistines were jealous of him, and the king sent him away in peace and told Isaac he had become even mightier than them. So, Isaac left and went to the Valley of Gerar and dwelt there. God continued to bless Isaac over and over again. Even when the Philistines had stopped up the wells that Isaac used, he would just move again to another location and set up a house and then have his servants dig new wells, and God would give water through the new wells. Eventually, the Philistines' made a covenant with Isaac to live in peace with him in the same land because they saw that no matter what they did to try and stop Isaac's flow of blessings from God, it would always be rendered useless. It is true if God be for you, who can be against you.

When we keep God's statutes and live our lives according to His commandments, we are assured to be successful in all we do. Our stock must be in God and His ways, so God's stock will most assuredly be in us. Therefore, the moral of this story is that when God takes stock in you, no weapon formed against you will ever prosper. What God has ordained no man can put a sunder.

There is no doubt that our future in the Lord is bright when we seek His wisdom for our lives; therefore, let us follow the old paths and where the good way is, and walk in them as it says in Jeremiah 6:16 so that we will be blessed of the Lord and receive our inheritance as promised to us through Abraham and Isaac. Let's take stock in each other so we can help one another overcome this world through the blessings of God. And let this encourage us to take stock in God's leadership as our guidance which produces all the resources, we need to accomplish His will for our lives.

In John 10:10, Jesus warns that the thief's only purpose is to steal, kill, and destroy. But He declares that His purpose is to bring life—life in abundance.

Thanks to the unwavering leadership of all our Bible ancestors who said yes to receiving God's stock so we could all prosper through His unwavering leadership to all generations now and forever. Amen.

Chapter 7

The Value of A Birthright

Have you ever wondered about the value of a birthright? I have. Reading the story of Esau and Jacob makes me see the importance of such matters. Esau takes his birthright lightly. However, Jacob and their mother do not. A birthright in those days was a special honor given to the firstborn son. He was to be blessed with a double portion of the family inheritance and given the honor of becoming the family leader. However, it was at his discretion whether he wanted to keep it in effect or not.

Esau was a hunter, an outdoor kind of person who smelled of animal skins and such. However, Jacob was a tent dweller who stayed close to home and enjoyed a softer life than being an outdoorsman. One day, Esau was out hunting and doing the outdoor stuff he loved, and was extremely hungry. He smelled Jacob's stew cooking and asked him if he could have some of his stew to eat. Jacob knew that his brother Esau did not value his birthright. He said yes and coached Esau into giving up his birthright to him. Esau was eager to give it up over simple hunger pangs. Not even thinking it through first, he said, "Look, I am about to die, so what is this birthright to me?" Then Esau sold his birthright to Jacob, not even thinking about the consequences that would come back to haunt him in the future over the subject matter.

Sometimes we can get caught up in the moment of making unwise decisions like Esau did with his birthright. That is why it is wise to seek God's counsel before making a rash decision that could alter your future and give into regret that cannot be reversed. When Esau found out that Isaac gave Jacob his firstborn blessing instead of him, Esau wept bitterly, and it was too late to reverse his unwise decision. Esau begged Isaac to give him a blessing anyway. And so, Isaac did but it was not as good as the blessing he had given to Jacob. Esau hated his brother after that incident.

Before Jacob left for his uncle's home in Haran, Isaac blessed him once more. Meanwhile, Esau vowed to kill his younger brother, even though it was his own fault for giving up his birthright, which now rightfully belonged to Jacob. The lesson we learn here is never to give up a birthright or any other blessings that the Lord has set in place for you or possibly your offspring. Making fast, wrong decisions can end up with dire consequences.

God's leadership reflects a secure future in our birthright He has given us through His Son, Jesus. So many times, we as God's children forget about the blessings that our Savior spoke over us before His death on the cross, and yet we can find ourselves willing to give them all up over sinful pleasures of all sorts, not giving thought of the cost Jesus went to secure our future in the Kingdom of Heaven.

The story of Esau and Jacob was a foreshadowing of the Son of God coming to redeem mankind. Where food stole the birthright of a man, God would use the Passover food to bring that birthright back. When Jesus did Passover with the disciples and blessed the bread and wine, He explained the symbolism of both to the disciples. In Matthew it says that Jesus gave thanks over the cup of wine and then said, *'Drink from it, all of you. For this is My blood of the new covenant, which is shed for many for the remission of sins. But I say to you; I will not drink of this fruit of the vine from now on until that day when I drink it new with you in My Father's kingdom' (Matthew 26:27).* Bam! It marked the moment He was securing our birthright in Heaven.

However, like Esau, there was one disciple named Judas Iscariot willing to sell his birthright for his own gain. He gave it away for 30 pieces of silver. It is amazing how a man can get caught up in the moment and give away the blessings of God without giving much thought to it, some hating the responsibility of their birthright as a child of God. All the while forgetting the price Jesus paid with His life so we could receive our kingdom rights now and not just when we die. Jesus came so that we could have life, and have it more abundantly, setting the pace for us on Earth as it is in Heaven.

Let us ponder upon the qualifying leadership our birthright has given us through God our Father, who has bestowed His blessings upon us throughout the ages for following His commandments. Our birthright as a citizen of Heaven comes with great responsibility, and therefore, we should not take it lightly that God has called us out, among others, to serve Him in all we do and think. May we, as citizens of Heaven, grasp the moment with our birthright in hand and seize the day and every hour while His salvation may be found, sharing it with those who are lost and heading on a fast track that dead ends to hell's fiery furnace.

There will be no time to hide behind someone or something with excuses when you see your brethren, our savior, coming in the distance because of the shame of refusing your birthright. Or will you boldly step forward and receive His greeting and redeem your birthright for the remission of your sins, knowing you did not give away or steal your birthright to receive the blessing of salvation? We must follow God's leadership and boldly serve our heavenly Father with gratefulness guarding our hearts against temptations that can affect our birthright. Only the blood of the Lamb can and will secure our birthright for all eternity. I am so glad Jesus took His birthright seriously. He truly received a double portion of His inheritance; He has been given honor and dominion over all the earth for ages to come. Amen.

Chapter 8

Staying the Course

Joseph was the eleventh son of Jacob and his father's favorite. His ten older brothers were extremely jealous of him and wanted to kill him. However, one of the brothers, Reuben, suggested instead, "Let's throw him into a pit." So they did; Rueben had plans later to come back and get him out of the pit and take him back to his father, Jacob. Unknowingly while Rueben was gone, the other brothers took Joseph and sold him to a caravan passing by and later, they sold Joseph to an officer in Pharaoh's army. Joseph lived in his master's house serving him. Although Joseph was now living in Egypt as a servant, he was still staying the course by continuing to let God guide him through his hardships. He kept his heart humble before the Lord and the young and ambitious Joseph, who used to be the bragger of how God was going to use him, learned to let God lift him up instead of himself with his own mouth.

God rewarded Joseph for his steadfastness. Joseph continued to let God be his leader and counsel for his life. God rewarded him for his quiet behavior and the wisdom he possessed before his master. God gave him great favor with all with who he came in contact to the point that even Pharaoh made him his right-hand man who could do whatever he wanted without consulting the King directly. The king trusted Joseph and his integrity to run his kingdom and those who lived in it. God was grooming Joseph for a very special moment in time for the region he lived in.

There was a famine coming to that region, and with God's leadership, guidance, and counsel, Joseph was able to tell Pharaoh what needed to be done before it happened. Pharaoh followed the instructions and had Joseph lead the people to prepare for the seven-year famine so they would have plenty of food and water during those seven years. Joseph was empowered with the wisdom of God, and not only did that region survive the famine, but they were able to sell their surplus to other regions around them.

Joseph would learn the true reason God had allowed him to go through all the hardships he did. One day during the famine period, Joseph's brothers showed up to buy wheat and other items that were needed to get them through the famine in their region. The brothers did not know that Joseph was their brother whom they had sold to the passing trade's caravan back when he was a boy. Joseph knew who they were and put them to some sneaky little test to see if they would eventually come clean with what they had done to him. However, God had trained Joseph so well during those separation years from his family to mirror His image and His attitude. So much so that during the event of helping his brothers get the food rations they needed to take back to their dad, Joseph had to excuse himself from his family so he could weep for joy that he would soon be reunited with his father and family.

Joseph ended up telling Pharaoh and his family who he was, and God honored every aspect of the situation. Joseph's family came and lived in Goshen near him. All Joseph ever wanted was to see his family again and be near his father, Jacob. While Joseph was living apart from his family during that season of unknown, Jacob had a 12th son named Benjamin who was Joseph's younger brother.

Long story short, out of Jacob came the twelve tribes of Israel. Before Jacob died, he had all his sons come into his room, and he spoke his final blessings to them. Now, Joseph's brothers, who had done their evil deeds against Joseph when he was young, were afraid that at the passing of their father's death, Joseph would take revenge against them.

However, Joseph was so happy to have his family back in his life that he told his brothers he forgave them, for if they had not done what they did, Joseph would not have been able to save all their lives and so many others during the seven-year famine. Wow! How powerful! He was willing to not blame anyone for his past hardships. Joseph chose to mimic his Father's leadership and reflect a clear sunshine day without clouds. Mirroring the Lord's love and mercy with compassion, being a shepherd designed by God, springing forth leadership as the beauty of the fresh morning dew on the ground, giving moisture to the thirsty souls of his brothers. How beautiful that moment in time must have been. Joseph had become a pillar of stone for his family that would never go away in their lifetime. Joseph was fruitful in all he accomplished because he trusted God with all the details of his life.

The value of Joseph's story shines forth a great picture of Yeshua staying the course through all his hardships on his journey to being the savior of the world. Yeshua became our daily bread and our living water so our souls would no longer live in a draught and famine place without God. It is like this: on the day you decide to accept Yeshua as your savior, He accepts you as family and forgives you of all your trespasses so you can live and not die and move to a new heavenly Goshen, a kingdom where we will never be separated from our heavenly Father ever again. Amen.

Chapter 9

The Bridle of the Tongue

This story has come about because I was searching in the Old Testament, and while doing so, I asked God to show me what this new chapter would be about and surprise! I came across a story in Numbers 12 about Miriam and Aaron not controlling their tongue. So, let's buckle up and dive into what God has planned for us on this new journey of how powerful or not our spoken words can be. It is a difficult subject to talk about for most people and even me, but the Father wants to address this issue, and so we shall.

Have you ever gossiped about someone you shouldn't have or spoken to a person in a wrongful manner and then regretted every moment of it afterward? I have and have had to repent of it many times. God wants to teach us about the bridle of the tongue because He knows it is a powerful tool that you can either tear down or build up someone with. Scripture says there is life and death in the tongue. No doubt that is a strong word from God and is a warning to use our words wisely with each other. We sometimes tend to jump the gun with others on our words spoken because God was excluded in the thought process of that word before it comes out of our mouth.

However, there is still hope for us all. If you have found yourself guilty of such sin, just stop and pause for a moment and ask God to forgive you and then commit to start including Him in the thoughtfulness of your words before you speak them out of your mouth. It's that simple and the rest will be history between you and your spoken words to others. God recently used a young man to help me see how important it is that I am true to my word and that I serve God well with my tongue. God used the young man's spoken words to set me on the right path to being even more careful with what I speak out of my mouth because I desire to be righteous before the Lord in all I do and say in my life. I want to influence him and others towards God in a positive manner so they, too, will desire to have a relationship with Him and live their life for Him.

So, on this journey, God had me come across Numbers 12, which is about Miriam and Aaron opposing Moses. Can you believe it! They actually opposed Moses' words spoken by God Himself. What were they thinking? It says,

> *[1] Then Miriam and Aaron spoke against Moses because of the Ethiopian woman whom he had married...[2] so they*

said, 'Has the Lord indeed spoken only through Moses? Has He not spoken through us also?' And the Lord heard it. [3] (Now the man Moses was very humble, more than all men who were on the face of the earth.)

[4] Suddenly, the Lord said to Moses, Aaron and Miriam, 'Come out, you three, to the Tabernacle of Meeting!' So the three came out. [5] Then the Lord came down in the pillar of cloud and stood in the door of the tabernacle, and called Aaron and Miriam. And they both went forward. [6] Then He said,

'Hear now My words: If there is a prophet among you, I, the Lord, make Myself known to him in a vision; [7] not so with my servant Moses; He is faithful in all my house. [8] I speak with him face to face, even plainly, and not in the dark sayings, and he sees the form of the Lord; why then were you not afraid to speak against my servant Moses?'

[9] So the anger of the Lord was aroused against them, and He departed. [10] And when the cloud departed from about the tabernacle, suddenly Miriam became leprous, as white as snow. Then Aaron turned toward Miriam, and there she was, a leper. [11] So Aaron said to Moses, 'Oh, my Lord! [12] Please do not lay this sin on us, which we have done foolishly and which we have sinned. Please do not let her be as one dead, whose flesh is half consumed when he comes out of his mother's womb!'

¹⁴ So Moses cried out to the Lord, saying, 'Please heal her, O God, I pray!'

¹⁴ Then the Lord said to Moses, 'If her father had but spit on her face, would she not be shamed seven days? Let her be shut out of the camp for seven days, and afterward she may be received again.' ¹⁵ So Miriam was shut out of the camp seven days and the people did not journey till Miriam was brought in again. ¹⁶ And afterward the people moved from Hazeroth and camped in the Wilderness of Paran. (Numbers 12:1-16)

God had mercy, and Miriam was healed because they repented of the sin of the tongue; having no bridle on the tongue can get you in trouble every time you speak loosely with it. The issue was that Aaron and Miriam could not find any fault with the leadership of Moses. The only thing they could find fault in was his Ethiopian wife, who was not Hebrew. Moses did not have a Hebrew wife because, remember, he was raised in Egypt. If God was not concerned about it, neither should they have been. Instead, they were using that issue to divert away from the real issue, which was they were jealous of Moses' relationship with God and how well he used that influence with the people they were leading across the desert to the promised land.

After I read the story of Miriam and Aaron, I bowed my head at my desk and repented again of all the words that have come out of the mouth, past or present, against anyone I know or do not know, and especially those whom God has chosen to be leaders teaching and guiding others to Him. I thank the Lord for His forgiveness, mercy and grace on this subject to all of us who know better in the Lord. The value of the lesson we learn here is that before we criticize someone else, we need to pause and discover our motive behind the criticism, whether it will be a constructive or destructive moment with our tongue. Because once you speak it out of your mouth, it cannot be retrieved.

From Proverbs 10, we can learn that the mouth of the righteous is a well of life, but violence covers the mouth of the wicked. Hatred stirs up strife, but love covers all sins. Wisdom is found on the lips of him who has understanding but not for one who does not. Wise people store up knowledge, but the mouth of the foolish is near destruction. Whoever hides hatred has lying lips, and whoever spreads slander is a fool. In the multitude of words, sin is not lacking, but the person who restrains his lips is wise. The tongue of the righteous is choice silver; the heart of the wicked is worth little. The lips of the righteous feed many, but the fools die for lack of wisdom. And in Proverbs15:1-4, it says that a soft answer turns away wrath, but a harsh word stirs up anger. The tongue of the wise uses knowledge rightly. But the mouth of fools pours forth foolishness. The eyes of the Lord are in every place, keeping watch on the evil and good. A wholesome tongue is a tree of life. But perverseness breaks the spirit.

The final word on this subject will be from Proverbs 21:23, which says, *"Whoever guards his mouth and tongue keeps his soul from troubles."* Amen.

Chapter 10

Careless Complaining

Careless complaining can get you in over your head if you do not use your words wisely. That is what happened to the Israelites when they were living in the desert after being set free by God from slavery in Egypt. Apparently, the Israelites were being sustained and fed manna from Heaven and that was not satisfying enough to them. They were looking back at all the fine fish, melons and such that had been in Egypt while in captivity. The Israelites complained to Moses that they wanted more meat in their diet. So, Moses went before the Lord and petitioned Him for more meat in the Israelite's diet. While he was at it, he complained to the Lord for more help to lead the people because the burden was too much for him alone, and he had no idea where to get enough meat to feed them all. Wow! Moses was second-guessing the Lord's ability to lead and to give enough meat to feed the children of Israel.

The Lord's anger was greatly aroused by Moses and the people that the Lord instructed Moses to pick seventy men who are known as elders of Israel and bring them to the tent of Tabernacles so that they may stand there with him and He would talk with all of them. *"I will take of the Spirit that is upon you and will put the same upon them; and they shall bear the burden of the people with you, that you may not bear it yourself alone"* (Numbers 11:17).

In Numbers 11:18-20, Moses was instructed to tell the people, *"Consecrate yourselves for tomorrow, and you shall eat meat, for you have wept in the hearing of the Lord, saying, 'Who will give us meat to eat? For it was well with us in Egypt.' Therefore, the Lord will give you meat, and you shall eat. You shall eat, not one day, nor two days, nor five days, nor ten days, nor twenty days, but for a whole month, until it comes out of your nostrils and becomes loathsome to you, because you have despised the Lord who is among you and have wept before Him, saying, 'Why did we ever come up out of Egypt?'"*

Moses still questioned the Lord about how they were to get the meat to feed everyone. And the Lord said to Moses, "Has the Lord's arm been shortened?" Now you shall see whether what I say will happen to you or not." So, Moses went out and told the people the words of the Lord, and he gathered the seventy men of the elders of the people and placed them around the Tabernacle. Then the Lord came down in the cloud, and spoke to him, and took of the Spirit that was upon him, and placed it on the seventy elders;

and it happened, when the Spirit rested upon them that they prophesied, although they never did so again.

After Moses and the seventy elders returned to camp, a strong wind came out from the Lord, and it brought quail from the sea and left those fluttering near the camp, about a day's journey on this side and about a day's journey on the other side, all around the camp. In other words, there was no escaping the quail falling from the sky. And the people stayed up all that day, all night, and all the next day, and gathered the quail (he who gathered least gathered at least ten homers), and they spread them out for themselves all around the camp. But while the meat was still in their teeth before it was chewed, the wrath of the Lord was aroused against the people, and the Lord struck the people with a very great plague. And the people that had complained had died and were buried in that same place they had yielded to craving. It's apparent their 'need' for more became sin because they already had plenty of what they needed to sustain them in the desert. No matter what God did for them, they never seemed to be thankful. They always seemed to want more and kept looking back with a heart and voice of ungratefulness, and all the while, the Lord was standing near and listening unknowingly to them. This means God is always listening even when we think He is not and even when our complaint is not to Him directly but to another person. Such as was with the Israelites to Moses. The Lord once again used His weather leadership to show the strong arm of the Lord is never shortened by man not having enough faith to believe that God can deliver us out of any situation or if the need calls to correct us out of the error of our ways.

How do we, as believers, define complaining in our own lives? Are there different levels of complaining, and if so, at what point do we stop and pause and be grateful for what we have been given and any increase God desires to give us beyond what we already have now? I don't know about you, but I'm taking a deep breath about it right now because I have been guilty of complaining about things I have no business complaining about as well. Let's pause for a second and ask the Lord to please forgive us for frivolous complaining, past or present. We must be still and know He is God and know He is in charge of all things great and small in our lives. I am thankful for the Lord's mercy to us as we continue to run the race with grace in this area of our lives. May we all do better from this day forth by not complaining and counting our blessings. Let's use the keys to the kingdom of Heaven to unlock new beginnings with the Lord as we learn to mirror His leadership skills with our lives. Next, we must learn to keep leaning into the Lord and trusting Him and not into our own understanding, but his, and He will give us the desires of our hearts.

"Bless the Lord, O my soul! O Lord my God, You are very great: You are clothed with honor and majesty, who cover Yourself with light as with a garment, who stretch out the heavens like a curtain. He lays the beams of His upper chambers in the waters, who makes the clouds His chariot, who walks on the wings of the wind, who

makes His angels spirits, His ministers a flame of fire" (Psalm 104:1-4).

Amen.

Volume 2

No Slumber Leadership

Chapter 1

His Watch

What I find interesting about God is that His watch includes no slumber. I see a vision of a watch on His wrist, and it does not include any hands for telling time. However, it says, "A day is like a thousand years."

Now, it was after Moses had passed away and God spoke to Joshua, the son of Nun who was Moses' assistant. He said, *"Go over the river Jordan, you and this entire people, to the land which I am giving to them—the children of Israel."*[1] God gave them a huge territory of land and said, *"No man shall be able to stand before you all the days of your life; as I was with Moses, so I will be with you. I will not leave you nor forsake you. Be strong and of good courage, for to this people you shall divide as inheritance the land*

---

[1] Joshua 1:2

which I swore to their fathers to give them."[2] God goes on to tell them to obey His book of laws and not to let them depart from their mouths, but He commanded them to meditate on it day and night, *"that you may observe to do according to all that is written in it. For then, you will make your way prosperous, and then you will have success. Have I not commanded you? Be strong and of good courage; do not be afraid, nor be dismayed, for the Lord your God is with you wherever you go."*[3]

Now, notice there are some key words that God is speaking to the children of Israel. God's leadership is very precise and intentional. So, when He asked us to follow His commands to the letter, we should. God does not have to keep proving Himself to His people that He is in command. What He is asking of them is to take charge of what He is giving them. Which means it was going to take faith to stand up and fight for the land they were being given. God was not just handing it over to them. He wanted to build their trust in Him 24/7. So, He set some guidelines up, and if you notice, He used the word *you* a lot in His sentences to them.

God wanted the Israelites to know His watch was without dials and He who watches over the Israelites does not sleep nor slumber. Their success would depend on them being faithful to

---

[2] Joshua 1:5-6
[3] Joshua 1:8-9

the command of the Lord. Joshua was now in charge of leading the Israelites across the Jordan into the promised land. However, before God allowed them to cross, they had to prepare provisions for themselves because, in three days, He tells them, "You will cross over the Jordan to go possess the land which the Lord your God is giving you to possess." Now, on the side they were residing on before crossing over the river, the Lord had given to the Reubenites, the Gadites, and half the tribe of Manasseh. The Lord was given all the tribes of Israel land so they could rest, but some of that land would be across the Jordan. God values rest, and He knew the Israelites had endured a long journey through the desert. Therefore, the warriors from certain tribes left their women, children, and livestock behind to cross over with the other men of valor, helping them take possession of the land where God also intended to give them rest. Once their mission was complete, they were instructed to return to their families in the land the Lord had given them.

The men of all the tribes agreed to follow the commandment of Joshua because they knew God was giving Joshua instructions on how the land across the river Jordan was going to be possessed. So much so that they would kill any man who did not follow Joshua's command. This was serious business, and the men knew God was the true commander. It was time to shut up or put up in their faith at this point, and there was no turning back. They only wanted to be strong and of good courage. Not looking to the left or right as God had instructed to do so.

Is there a battle you are trusting and believe God to win for you? If so, we can know sincerely His watch over us is not without care and love for us. He desires to give us all He has promised us through our ancestors and, most importantly, His Son, Jesus the Messiah. Are you standing on a promise the Lord has said He would do for you? What has been your part to receive it? Like the Israelites, there were guidelines they had to follow for it to happen.

Psalm 1:1-3 says,

> [1] *Blessed is the man who walks not in the counsel of the ungodly, nor stands in the path of sinners, nor sits in the seat of the scornful;* [2] *but his delight is in the law of the Lord, and His law he mediates day and night.* [3] *He shall be like a tree planted by the rivers of water that bring forth its fruit in its season, whose leaf also shall not wither, and whatever he does will prosper.*

Amen.

Chapter 2

The Need to Spy

Sometimes, we may feel the need to spy on the project God is calling us to complete. Joshua sent two men to spy out the land and the city of Jericho before they were to be given both land and city. He wanted to be completely prepared for any unforeseen issue with the people who dwelled in that area and in Jericho. The men spying made friends with a harlot by the name of Rehab and lodged there. She helped hide them from the king of Jericho and pretended she did not know who they were and said that they had sneaked out at night when the city gate was being closed.

What is interesting is that while the men spied on the city from the rooftop of her house, she said to them,

> *⁹ I know the Lord has given you the land, that the terror of you has fallen on us, and that all the inhabitants of the land are fainthearted because of you. ¹⁰ For we have heard*

how the Lord dried up the water of the Red Sea for you when you came out of Egypt, and what you did to the two kings of the Amorites who were on the other side of the Jordan, Sihon and Og, whom you utterly destroyed. [11] And as soon as we heard these things, our hearts were melted; neither did there remain any more courage in anyone because of you, for the Lord your God, He is God in heaven and above and on earth beneath. (Joshua 2:9-11)

You see, God had a plan and made sure the news of the Israelites having His favor was spread ahead of them so that the inhabitants of the land had knowledge to fear the Lord and those He protected. Therefore, that information made Rehab wise to know when to make a deal with the spies to save her family from the coming destruction upon Jericho. She made an oath with them she would be true to her word and would help them and never reveal who they were or what they were planning.

What we learn from this story is that we can apply it to our walk with the Lord. When God has called you to lead, do not be afraid to be prepared to spy out the land or learn more about the task He is giving you. It can be considered wise to do so, so that you know just what you are up against to advance with unknown circumstances that may occur during the process, even while you wait upon the Lord for the next move. Like Joshua, we must be ready and willing to know what our next move will be once the

Lord releases the information, we need to move forward on a project He has commissioned us to do. Just like Joshua, we must learn to lead with good preparation and encouragement to those who will be involved in the movement of God with us on the subject matter. God is the one who will make you successful if you have yielded all your plans to Him. He will make your way straight, and He will leave no stone unturned for you to complete the task ahead of you.

Now, there are two sides to the coin; it is not always necessary to spy to gain insider knowledge if your faith has reached a level of trust in the Lord that does not require spying on the land or the task at hand, He has commissioned you to do. The battle was already won for the Israelites, regardless of sending in the spies.

I know a friend who spied out the land he desired for at least 18 years and kept praying over that land, and now he and his family own that property. So, never give up when God has spoken a promise to you. Stay strong and have the courage to believe God will bring it to pass. Know what your part is in bringing the promises God has made to you to reality and be diligent, staying focused, trusting God, and not looking to the left or the right so you do not add confusion or disbelief, making it harder to receive the blessings promised.

Psalm 5:11-12 says,

¹¹ But let all those rejoice who put their trust in You; let them ever shout for joy, because You defend them; Let

those also who love Your name be joyful in You. ¹² *For You, O Lord will bless the righteous; with favor, You will surround him as with a shield.*

Chapter 3

The Living God

Joshua reminded the Israelites that crossing over the Jordan River to the promised land during its flood season was going to be okay and that the living God who brought them across the Red Sea would do the same here for them as He did with Moses. He had all the people cleanse spiritually, physically, and mentally for three days before they were to cross over the Jordan to possess the land. He wanted them all to be prepared with pure hearts before the living God of Israel.

Joshua told them that in three days, the Levite priest carrying the Ark of the Covenant would step and touch the edge of the river, and it would stop the river flowing and dry it up so the Israelites could cross over it safely. But before Joshua would let the men cross over the river, he had them stop and listen to his words on what was about to happen. He lifted the name of the living God of all the earth and Heaven. Afterward, the Levite priest carried the Ark of the Covenant to the center of the river and stood with it while all the Israelites crossed over on the dry riverbed.

Like Joshua and his men, it is sometimes especially important for us to slow down and prepare with the Lord's counsel before we rush in to do the job, He has called us to. Planning and knowing just how the Lord wants you to do what He has called you to do will bring a higher rate of success with less chance of failure. Even though Joshua's men were anxious to cross over the river and get the job done, Joshua knew they needed to slow their roll and be still and know God was in charge and all they needed to have was patience and trust in the one who had sent them here in this moment and time in history, for they were all born for a time such as this.

The Ark of the Covenant was a very important tool the Lord would have them use because it contained the Ten Commandments: Aaron's staff that was actually growing leaves out of it and a gold jar with manna from Heaven that had sustained the Israelites while wandering in the desert for 40 years. I love how God had the Israelites put His direct spoken Word of the Ten Commandments written on stone inside the Ark. Because God is our rock and refuge, and His care for us is real, and it is written in stone by Abba Father Himself. God is an amazing leader and needs us to understand that His wisdom is in His spoken Word. Hebrews 4:12 says,

*For the Word of God is living and powerful, and sharper
than any two-edged sword, piercing even to the division
of soul and spirit, and of joints and marrow, and is a
discerner of the thoughts and intents of the heart.*

Can you see now why it was important for the Israelites to repent and cleanse themselves in every area of their life for three days before they crossed over in front of the Ark with God's living Word inside of it? It is important for us to know the Ark was powered by God's living Word and that is why no one could touch it and had to follow behind it at a safe distance. The power of His Word abiding in the Ark is what commanded the river to stop flowing upstream, not the container it abided in. I have heard so many commentaries on the Ark and how powerful it was. All I can say is, of course, it was! God's living Word was housed in it.

Then, there was Aaron's staff, which was a symbol of God's rod of righteousness. Isaiah 11:1 says,

*There shall come forth a Rod from the stem of Jesse, and
a branch shall grow out of his roots.*

This was a representation of the messiah that would come from the remnant of the Israelites. The rod of Jesse arrived with righteousness through the heritage of a gold jar filled with manna from Heaven which was a reminder the Lord sustained them, and He was bringing them into the land of milk and honey. By doing so, He was setting the pace for the world's future and out of Jesse Usher in Yeshua, the Messiah who would become God in the flesh and be the bread of life from Heaven to sustain them in spirit and truth. Therefore, setting the Israelites future up for success in the land they were possessing across the Jordan River.

God was designing an everlasting covenant with the three items that were placed in the Ark. The items represented something of greater value that would become a metaphor for what was coming through Yeshua, the Messiah. It is exciting to know when we put our trust in the living God of all the universe, He will always have our best interest at heart because His leadership is impeccable and does not guide us to set us up for failure but success.

Chapter 4

Memorial Stones

It was Harvest time when Joshua and the 40,000 men of valor crossed over the Jordan River to possess the land. The Levite priest stood in the middle of the river while they did so with the Ark of the Covenant. Once all the men had made it across safely, the Lord instructed Joshua to take one man from each tribe, which was a total of twelve men and have them each carry a stone large enough upon their shoulders to the center of the river where the priest stood with the Ark and stack them up on top of each other as a memorial to the children of Israel that the Lord cut off the waters of the Jordan so they could cross over to the promised land and that all the peoples of the earth may know the hand of the Lord, that it is mighty, that you may fear the Lord your God forever. So, when they are children, ask them what the stones mean; they can tell them the importance of making the memorial, and it was to remain there forever.

God is such a personable leader and thoughtful with all His plans for us. After the men of valor crossed over the Jordan, God did not have the Israelites rush to siege the land. Instead, He slowed them down to rest. He wanted them to utilize the time as a reflection of where they had come from and where they are in the present. God was able to use this rest time to have them recount their step across the river and the time they spent in the desert by placing a stone memorial in the center of the river. So, they and future generations would live in reverence for the past and future. Not forgetting, God made their enemies fear them because His favor was upon them. In doing so, the people of all the earth would hear of His favor on them and fear the mightiness of the Lord, too.

What a timely message for the USA and other countries in modern times. America has allowed the Ten Commandments to be removed from public schools and courthouses by evildoers. Not to mention other memorials in the USA that have been removed, and now, we, the people, are suffering at the hands of those who do not believe in God's leadership or His plan for us to live in freedom. They want to remove the entire memorials that remind us of the good things God did for us in this country and of the men who first led this country into freedom and to serve God freely without the boundaries of evil leaders.

God has set the pace for mankind over and over throughout the Bible with His leadership skills and mighty power, and yet somehow evil men want to try and force the entire world to forget

God's mightiness and His love and care for all generations. If memorials were not important, then the evil doers of this world would not be trying so hard to destroy them and steal our freedoms and kill innocent unborn children while still in the womb, which are new generations that can carry on truth to the next generations. Memorials are important to God. If not, He would not have laid the groundwork for such matters in the middle of the Jordan River.

When I think of those memorial stones and the purpose they stand for in the Jordan River, it reminds me of a verse in Psalms:

> *Be my strong refuge, to which I may resort continually; you have given the commandment to save me, for you are my rock and my fortress. Deliver me, O my God, out of the hand of the wicked, out of the hand of the unrighteous and cruel man, for you are my hope, O Lord God; You are my trust from my youth. By you, I have been upheld from birth; you are He who took me out of my mother's womb. My praise shall be continually of You. (Psalm 71:3-6)*

God never just has you do something for nothing; there will always be a plan behind it. So, the next time God slows your roll, do not fuss or be upset about it. Just seek out His wisdom on the subject, and He will gladly explain it to you just as He did Joshua and the children of Israel.

Let us be reminded of Psalm 71:17-18, which says:

O God, You have taught me from my youth, and to this day, I declare Your wondrous works. Now also when I am old and gray headed, O God, do not forsake me, until I declare Your strength to this generation, Your power to everyone who is to come.

Therefore, let us take up our cross daily as a memorial and follow the Lord and share about what Yeshua did for us on the cross so that we declare His salvation and God's strength to this generation and His power to everyone who is to come. Amen.

Chapter 5

A Second Generation

After the memorial stones were in place in the Jordan River, the Priest brought the Ark across to the promised land with Joshua and the 40,000 men of valor. And when the Ark was removed out of the Jordan River, its banks were flooded again with its water. A second generation had been chosen to live in the new land of promise.

While the men rested, they waited for instructions from Joshua to hear whatever the next step was from the Lord. The Lord told Joshua that he should make flint knives for himself and circumcise the sons of Israel again the second time. So, Joshua did as he was instructed and made the flint knives and circumcised the sons of Israel. All the men who had come out of Egypt had been circumcised, but those who had been born in the wilderness in those 40 years had not. Now that all the original men of valor were no longer alive, it would be their sons who would be allowed to enter the land of milk and honey. Then Joshua circumcised their sons, who God had raised in their place, for they had not been circumcised on the way to Israel.

So it was, when they had finished circumcising all the people they stayed in their places in the camp until they were healed. Then the Lord spoke to Joshua, "This day I have rolled away the reproach of Egypt from you. The name of this place is called Gilgal[4] to this day.

Once again, the Lord is magnifying His leadership role over the Israelites by keeping His promise of delivering the children of Israel to the promised land even though it was a second generation of young men who were the children of the men who started the journey with Moses out of Egypt. They, too, could have completed the journey. Still, unfortunately, their disobedience banned their entrance into the promised land.

What is amazing is that this incident shows that God will always keep His promises to us regardless of if we fail to keep our end of the bargain. God does not ask much of us other than that we follow His commands and statues to the letter of which He has instructed. The wonderful thing is we now have the grace to run the race with the help of the Comforter, the Holy Spirit. God's

---

[4] The word "Gilgal" comes from the Hebrew גִּלְגָּל and means "circle" or "rolling."

Word is clear and precise in following His instructions to receive all His goodness and favor all the days of our life.

Humility is a good place to start because pride comes before the fall. Kneel when in doubt and seek the Father's forgiveness of any sin that may be holding up your blessings promised to you. By circumcising your heart and renewing a right spirit in yourself, you will allow God's blessings to be released to you like never before. The floodgates of Heaven will open and overflow to the banks of your life. I will tell you this: the experience of my own repentance and circumcising of my heart before the Lord has yielded so many wonderful blessings since I was a child because my mother taught me to love and obey the Lord. I have no complaints about my life and how it has turned out. I am blessed indeed.

Let the wisdom of the Lord instruct us all the days of our life. Let us not look to the left or right but look straight ahead, gaining courage and hope through the Lord of Heaven and Earth, who holds the future in His hands. He is ready to lead us and provide for us at any given time. Our part is to know how to receive the promises of God. So, when we say yes to Him to lead as our Commander and Chief, it will set our future up for success, not failure. A circumcised heart to the Lord sets the pace to follow His standards, and it blows the water right out of our path and dries the ground we are walking on so we do not slip because we will have His favor to complete our journey in the fullness of the Lord's blessings. Thank God a second generation of Israelites was willing to carry the torch for future generations, which includes us, so we can learn to do the same.

Psalm 51:10-12 says:

[10] Create in me a clean heart, O God, and renew a right spirit within me. [11] Do not cast me away from Your presence, and do not take Your Holy Spirit from me. [12] Restore to me the joy of your salvation and uphold me by Your generous Spirit.

Chapter 6

Passover

It was now spring, and all the young men of Israel from the second generation had been circumcised. It was also the season of Passover, marking the first time the Israelites would celebrate the festival in the land of Israel. They were still camped at Gilgal, where they observed Passover at twilight on the plains of Jericho. The day after Passover, they ate the produce of the land—unleavened bread and parched grain—on the very same day. Then, the manna ceased on the day after they had eaten the produce of the land, and the children of Israel no longer had manna from Heaven, but they ate the food of the land of Canaan that year. It was now time for the Israelites to go back to providing food for themselves by working the land to produce food for their nutriment. God would no longer have to give them manna from Heaven to survive because the new land had plenty of resources to provide for them. Once again it proves that when it is God's will, your journey will lack nothing to complete it.

The first time Israel had Passover was when they left Egypt in a hurry, and the Lord had told them to eat their food standing. What a new difference this was for the Israelites to eat their Passover food, rest and relax, and prepare for the takeover of the land of milk and honey. The celebration was to remind them of God's mighty miracles He did for them while in the desert. God had designed it that way so a fresh new beginning with a second generation of Israelites would observe the first Passover in the promised land, which would produce a new way of life for them. A new life the Lord had promised their forefathers, and now, here, a new generation was beginning their freedom in a new land called Israel.

This Passover had a new meaning for the children of Israel; it meant never having to live in slavery or have their children born in slavery. The possibilities would be innumerable. They could worship the Lord in freedom and not be in danger of being killed for believing in Him. They wanted God to be their leader. One day, Joshua was walking near Jericho and lifted his eyes and saw a man standing opposite of him with his sword drawn in his hand. Joshua went and asked him," Are you for us or for our adversaries?" So, the man said, "No, but as Commander of the army of the Lord, I have now come."

And Joshua fell on his face to the earth and worshiped, and said to him, "What does my Lord say to His servant?" Then the Commander of the Lord's army said to Joshua, "Take your sandals off your feet, for the place where you stand is holy." And Joshua did so.

Wow, this is so powerful. God understood that Joshua needed clear guidance on how to secure victory with Him. As the time approached for Joshua to lead his army against Jericho, an angel appeared with specific instructions on how to carry out the siege. God had a precise plan, and it was crucial for Joshua and his warriors to follow it exactly.

Jericho was tightly shut up; none went in or out because of their fear of the Israelites. It was one of the oldest cities in the world of its time. The walls of the city had fortified walls that were twenty-five feet high and twenty feet thick walls. The soldiers of Jericho could see for miles from the high walls and could see anyone approaching from a long distance. The dynamics of the massive city walls must have looked almost impossible for any army to sneak attack or bust through its city walls to siege it. However, this was not going to be just any army coming to overtake them. Now, there was a new King in town, and His name was I AM, and He was in command of the army of Israel that would soon be attacking Jericho. The Lord wanted to destroy Jericho because it was a city full of sin like Sodom. God was driving out the unclean from Israel.

The Lord told Joshua to have the men of war march around the city of Jericho for six days, once only each day in silence; no noise was to come out of their mouths. Then, return to camp and do the same each day. Then, on the seventh day, march seven times around it and remain silent until Joshua gives the command to shout. The men of valor were ready now to march to Jericho. God had spent 40 years training the Israelites and conditioning them to obey His command for this very moment. The men of valor were steady in their trust in the Lord, prepared to walk by faith, not by sight. I am sure they were thinking at this point that no matter what happens, nothing is going to stop us, for we trust in the Lord. What a great charge for our faith in modern times. Can you imagine what the people of Jericho were thinking as they watched 40,000 men of war march around their city in silence?

And so, as it goes on the seventh day, on the seventh time around the walls of Jericho, the Israelites come to a stop, and the seven priests blow the horns, and right on que Joshua gave the command to shout, and they all did so. Joshua said, "Shout for the Lord has given you the city!" And the walls fell flat! The city of Jericho did not stand a chance because God's living Word was marching around the outer walls of Jericho; the Word was judgment against the people in the inner walls of its city. God's Word is powerful!

It just goes to show that a wall or any other hidden place is the wicked choice to hide from God. No man can. Our God El, Roi, is all-seeing.

What an amazing journey the Israelites had taken from Egypt to the land of milk and honey. Truly, God was with them. His favor was upon them. What a wonderful Passover to remember for all time. Their first Passover, they were fleeing from their enemy in fear, and this new season, their enemies feared them, and they would be the conquerors so they could live in freedom.

The lesson God wants us to learn from this powerful story is that we are all to have a Passover season in our lives because it reminds us of the desert times we have lived and of the goodness of God sustaining us through those times. It shows us how His favor to us can cause our enemy's hearts to faint.

God is a leader who can outwit the enemy and win the battle for us even before we approach the battlefield. Who can know the thoughts of God? Our plans are not His plans. Seeking the Lord's counsel is very advisable because He desires to give us only His absolute best. We are His children, and He always wants to give us His favor because, with it, our enemies will fear God because He is on our side. I AM bows down to no one and wants us to live under His blessings of protection because the battle belongs to the Lord. Worry can harvest sin because it can make you not trust the Lord for a favorable outcome or cause you not to seek His counsel on the subject matter.

God wants to restore us from our past so we can live in the present refreshed and rejuvenated, ready to siege the day so we can tell a new generation of His mighty works. The mightiest of His acts is that He loves us and desires to bless His children.

Psalm 1:1-2 says:

¹ Blessed is the man who walks not in the counsel of the ungodly, nor stands in the path of sinners, nor sits in the seat of the scornful: ² but his delight is in the law of the Lord.

Chapter 7

A Lost Battle

Have you had the confidence that you will win every battle set before you? However, instead you end up facing a lost battle and then have to reevaluate the lost opportunity to win, to understand better why it was lost. Joshua had to do the same thing when he and his men lost the first battle against the city of Ai. Joshua sent out spies to find out how large an army they had and the people that dwelled there. The spies came back and said there was no need to send out more than three thousand troops. They commented that the city of Ai was small, and that they should be able to overthrow it with ease. And so, Joshua sent out a small regiment of men to take Ai.

The men Joshua sent went to the gate of Ai and ended up fleeing from Ai's men protecting the gate. Ai's army chased the Israelites a long distance, and thirty-five of their men perished. After the Israelite's troops returned to camp and told Joshua of their defeat at Ai, Joshua tore his clothes. He and the elders of Israel threw dust on their heads and went before the Ark of the Covenant and bowed down to the Lord and Joshua cried out to Him and asked why they lost the battle at Ai. When He had promised them that they would win all their battles in the land, and now the inhabitants in the land would not fear them, and they would devour them.

> *¹⁰ So the Lord said to Joshua: 'Get up! Why do you lie thus on your face? ¹¹ Israel has sinned, and they have also transgressed My covenant which I commanded them. For they have even taken some of the accursed things, and have both stolen and deceived; and they have also put it among their own stuff.*

> *¹² Therefore the children of Israel could not stand before their enemies, but turned their backs before their enemies, because they have become doomed to destruction. Neither will I be with you anymore, unless you destroy the accursed from among you.*

> *¹³ Get up, sanctify the people, and say, "Sanctify yourselves for tomorrow, because thus says the Lord God of Israel: 'There is an accursed thing in your midst, O Israel; you cannot stand before your enemies until you take away the accursed thing from among you.'"" (Joshua 7:10-13)*

So, Joshua followed the Lord's instructions. The Lord had each tribe present themselves before Him, one by one. The Lord then declared, "The man who took the accursed objects will be burned along with all his belongings." As the process continued, a man named Achan came forward and confessed to Joshua that he had indeed sinned against the Lord, the God of Israel. He had taken spoils from the battle of Jericho in defiance, and he had hidden the items in his tent and buried silver coins in the ground within his tent as well. Once Joshua confirmed he had done what he said he did, he followed the instructions of the Lord and had Achan, and his entire family and animals stoned to death. Then, his household items and their dead bodies were burned, thus removing the curse from the children of Israel.

It was important for Joshua and the children of Israel to deal ruthlessly with the sin that had been committed against the Lord because they had made a covenant with the Lord to follow His instructions and live by His statutes. A change of heart had to take place immediately. Suppose they wanted God to continue to keep His promises to them by letting them win their battles all the time. The Israelites were a team; they were family. They acted as one unit. So, if one sinned against the instructions of the Lord, they all failed and sinned. No compromise could be tolerated when it came to disobedience against the Lord.

God had kept His promises to them, and now the Israelites acting as one vehicle to overcome the enemies in the promised land had a nail in one of its tires. The air was slowly leaking out of their grace of protection. This proves how sin can sneak into our families' lives through selfish, greedy thoughts that breed generational sin that brings curses upon ourselves and those we care about. Sin bans us from God's care and protection. When God reveals the sin in our lives, we must act swiftly and wisely to remove it immediately so that a lost battle is not our destiny.

God's leadership advice is *humility*. Because it keeps us grounded and can ensure our destiny is filled with blessings and not curses. Satan comes to steal, kill and destroy us because he himself has been banned from God's good pleasures. Satan is sneaky and tries to appear wise with cunning words to deceive you away from the love and care of God. I recently heard a pastor say that Satan is afraid of man because we are created in the image of God. Therefore, that is why Satan must be sneaky in his attack against us because when he looks at us, he is looking at God. It makes sense to me. So, you see, we have more power than we think to overcome sin. Not only can we ask to be forgiven of our sins and be forgiven, but we are created in His image, the God who threw Satan and one-third of the angels out of Heaven. Powerful indeed! We cannot serve two masters; we will either love one or hate the other. Purging sin from among us can take a stance against the unseen evils of this world. James 4:7 says to resist the devil, and he will flee from you.

Once Joshua and the children of Israel set things right with the Lord, it brought righteousness back into the camp, and the sin Achan had committed was forgiven. Now the Lord was ready to restore victory to them, and so it was Joshua who resent the men of valor back to Ai, and they utterly destroyed them and their city. The Lord allowed them this time to take the spoils of the city and the livestock.

After winning the battle, Joshua built altars to the Lord on Mount Ebal, as Moses had commanded in the Book of the Laws that the altar had to be built out of whole stone that no man had wielded with an iron tool. They offered burnt offerings to the Lord and sacrificed peace offerings.

Next, Joshua blesses the people, and he reads all the words of the law. There was not a word of all that Moses commanded which Joshua did not read before all the assembly of Israel and the strangers living among them. He did this to renew their covenant with God.

Once we make things right with the Lord and repent of what we did wrong. Things will start working out to our advantage. The Lord is faithful to keep His promises to us. He is a Father who loves to bless His family. Let us learn from God's wisdom that we must deal ruthlessly with the sin in our lives, or sin will deal ruthlessly with us.

Psalm 97:10-12 says,

¹⁰ You who love the Lord; hate evil! He preserves the souls of His saints; He delivers them out of the hand of the wicked. ¹¹ Light is sown for the righteous, and gladness for the upright in heart. ¹² Rejoice in the Lord, you righteous, and give thanks in the remembrance of His holy name.

Chapter 8

Be Not Deceived

In 1 Corinthians 15, Paul writes:

> *33 Do not be deceived: evil company corrupts good habits.*
> *34 Awake to righteousness, and do not sin, for some do not*
> *have the knowledge of God. I speak this to your shame. (1*
> *Corinthians 15:33-34)*

Scripture warns us to choose our friends carefully because the way of the wicked leads them astray (Proverbs 12:26). This happened to Joshua when his neighbors intentionally deceived him.

> *3 But when the inhabitants of Gibeon heard what Joshua*
> *had done to Jericho and Ai, 4 they worked craftily and*
> *went and pretended to be ambassadors. And they took old*
> *sacks on their donkeys, old wineskins torn and mended,*
> *5 old and patched sandals on their feet, and old garments*
> *on themselves; and all the bread of their provision was dry*

*and moldy. ⁶ And they went to Joshua, the camp at Gilgal,
and said to him and to the men of Israel, 'We have come
from a far country; now, therefore, make a covenant with
us.' ⁷ Then the men of Israel said to the Hivites, 'Perhaps
you dwell among us; so how can we make a covenant with
you?'*

*⁸ But they said to Joshua, 'We are your servants.' And
Joshua said to them, 'Who are you, and where do you
come from?' ⁹ So they said to him: 'From a very far
country your servants have come, because of the name of
the Lord your God; for we have heard of His fame, and all
that He did in Egypt, ¹⁰ and all He did to the two kings of
the Amorites who were beyond the Jordan…." (Joshua
9:3-10)*

And so, the Gibeons went on to deceive Joshua and his men
with a sad story of how bad their provisions were and how bad
their clothes and sandals looked. I mean to tell you the enemy
went all out to fool the Israelites. The leaders of Israel were now
caught in the net of deceit because of choosing their allies
unwisely.

Unbelievably, the men of Israel took some of their provisions
and gave them the Gibeon's and did not bother to ask counsel
from the Lord if they should or not. So, Joshua made peace with
them and made a covenant with them to let them live, and the
rulers of the congregation swore to them. At the end of three days,

after they had made a covenant with the Gibeons, Joshua heard they were their neighbors who dwelt near them. And so, it was the children of Israel who could not destroy them because of the oath Joshua and the elders of Israel promised not to harm but to make peace with them.

Now, it places the Israelites in an awkward position with their enemies. The children of Israel were angry that Joshua and the elders did not seek God's counsel on whether to make a peace covenant or not with the Gibeon's. In fact, they were so angry they wanted to march and kill them all and destroy their city as well. But they could not because of the oath their leadership took before the Lord God of Israel not to bring harm to them, therefore making a peace treaty with them.

Sometimes, leaders or individuals can make a hasty decision that can affect others besides themselves because of not seeking wise counsel from the Lord. It would appear that Joshua and the elders thought there was no need to seek the advice of the Lord, who had brought them there in the first place. You would have thought that they had learned their lesson with the first battle lost to Ai because of the deception of one of their men. Unfortunately, they did not gain any wisdom from the Ai loss. Now, here, they had to defend the enemy from their own people. What an embarrassment and shame it must have brought upon the leadership of Israel at that very moment they realized they had been so easily deceived.

Is there something in your life that you were easily deceived by, and now you have to eat crow because of it? It's a situation where you have to stand by your word and endure the consequences of the mistake you have made. Well, that is what happened to Joshua and the elders of Israel because they made an oath even though their enemy deceived them. They still had to honor the oath because God said oaths are binding, and they knew that breaking the oath was not an option. So, they had to face their shame head-on and once again back up and repent of not asking God what to do with the strangers who had used deceit to get under their good graces.

The pitfall of shame cannot keep us bound, but God can release us of shame once we ask Him to forgive us of that mistake. You may still have to live with the consequences of it like the Israelites did, but you can still overcome it with the guidance and care of the Lord's help so that you do not repeat the vicious cycle that it can cause in your life. God's leadership is clear-cut, and he lays out guidelines to follow so we have less of a chance to fail in our walk with Him while we continue to grow up in His kingship. His grace can and will forgive us because His banner over us is love, and it will cover a multitude of sins, regardless of the shame that brought us to that point in the first place. So, renew your vow to the Lord and ask forgiveness of whatever you need to and then put the rest back into His care plan and simple. Amen.

Chapter 9

The Ability

Suppose God gave you the ability to speak to the sun and moon to be still so you could accomplish something that was urgent for that day. Would you? Joshua leads the way for us who are of faith to do just that. It says there has not been a day like that since. But could there be if we in the faith had the ability to do so; of course, we could if our faith is intact even to that of a mustard seed. Oh, but wait! More importantly is our relationship with the Lord intact to do so as well? For if we do, nothing is impossible with God, for we can all things through Christ who strengthens us.

The ability to call the sun and moon to be still is an incredible miracle that Joshua had the authority to do because his leader was God, and he had a close enough relationship with Him that God spoke to Joshua directly as He had done with Moses. Joshua 10:12 states:

¹² Then Joshua spoke to the Lord in the day when the Lord delivered up the Amorites before the children of Israel, and he said in the sight of Israel:

'Sun, stand still over Gibeon; and moon, in the Valley of Aijalon.' ¹³ So the sun stood still. And the moon stopped.

Wow! Can you imagine the shock it put on the earth and its atmosphere? Maybe that is why large hail stones were falling from Heaven because the moon's gravitational pull to keep them in orbit in the sky caused them to fall. Of course, I am not a scientist, and I am just speculating about what could have happened. However, it is something to consider and stirs up curiosity to go and search the subject out some more.

What I find interesting about this story is that the reason for the war against the Amorites is that the king of Jerusalem had called on the help of four other kings in that area to come and attack the Gibeons because they had made a peace treaty with the Israelites and so Gibeon called on Joshua and his army to come and protect them from being harmed by the five kings. Well, because of the oath Joshua and the elders of Israel had taken to protect them, they responded immediately to come and rescue them. Needless to say, it was in the plan from the beginning because what was meant for bad turned out to be in Israel's favor for making peace with the Gibeons because it made it much easier for Israel to overtake the five kings and their cities, which grouped them in one area, given the Israelites the ability destroy all of them easier instead of individual cities. I am so glad God was able to turn the deceit of the Gibeons into something good for Joshua and his army. On that day, the sun and moon were called to stand still.

Another thing I noticed about this story is that the five kings went and hid in a cave because of their fear of losing their armies, and now they had to face the consequences of their actions of attacking Gibeon, who was a friend of Israel. God said He will bless those who bless Israel and will curse those who curse Israel. Joshua took those five kings and killed them and then hung them on a tree, then in the evening, took them down and buried their bodies in the cave the kings had hidden in and afterward laid large stones in from of the entrance.

Now, this is getting even more interesting. Yeshua was hung on a tree for our transgressions, and in the evening, his body was laid in a cave for burial, and then a large stone was rolled in front of the entry. The symbolic picture is amazing because Yeshua chose to lay down His life for us because being hung on a tree was a symbol of being cursed. Now, we who have accepted Yeshua in our hearts can be freed from the curse of sin and death. God was planning our future even in the days of Joshua. Yeshua was there watching with the Father as Israel was being given the land of milk of honey. The word with Joshua and Yeshua is the living Word that brought the sun and moon to a standstill so the battle could be won. Amazing repeatedly how Ancient of Days was speaking in the beginning days of Israel, acquiring the land that He loves so greatly that He was preparing the world to be saved from their curses.

Be still and know that God is. When in doubt, be still and step into the eye of the storm where His stillness is. His salvation for mankind is peace, and in that peace, we will find the ability to have faith to call things into His stillness, which is His quietness right before the battle is won and if the Lord be for us, who can be against us. Amen.

Chapter 10

A New Season

It was a new phase, a new season of the beginning of the end for Israel. Though Joshua was now old, somewhere between 80 and 100, God was still not finished with him. He still had a few years left to manage the tribes to resolve land dividing and so forth.

It was time for Israel to be in complete control of the land of milk and honey, which needed to be divided and allotted to each tribe. Joshua disbanded the army of Israel and sent them all back to their tribes. Each tribe had to go out and spy on the land they wanted and then come back to Joshua and let him know the details of the territory they desired to possess. And then he would bless them to receive the land and to go out and drive out their enemies that still occupied those areas. God was giving them peace to live in the land. However, not all the tribes drove out their enemies. Instead, they disobeyed the Lord and allowed some of them to continue to live among them and serve them, which later would cause issues with those remaining in their land.

The Israelites got compliant and lazy because they did not have all of Israel to help them fight their battles; they decided it was not worth the effort to complete the win to have total peace as the Lord had promised them. They lost their encouragement and quit depending on God to help them destroy their enemies to drive them out of the land. The Israelites forgot that the battle was already won and that a battle of any sort requires trust, faith, encouragement, and the strength to endure to receive that which the Lord was giving them. In the same way, we who are believers can find ourselves in the same predicament when we forget to keep God's promises in our hearts.

Joshua had grown old, but it did not stop him from leading Israel into receiving their inheritance. Israel was accustomed to having a large regiment to help win all their battles, but they forgot it was not the strength of their army but the strength of the Lord's hand that let them win all their battles, past and present.

Now it was that Joshua sent the tribe of Reuben, Gad and half of Manasseh back across the Jordan to their people, and he told them to share their riches with them. And so, they did. However, after getting back home to their land, they built an altar to the Lord. They made it so it would be a sign between them and the other tribes across the river on the west side that they would always serve the Lord because He was God. The children of Israel almost came and destroyed them because they did not want to anger the Lord; because they were not to build an altar unless God had told them to, and so they feared the consequences of it. What a great lesson to learn that it is important to never rush ahead of the Lord without consulting Him first.

Joshua had to use his leadership of expertise with wisdom to decide the case. After talking to the three tribes about the altar and why it was built. Joshua ruled in favor of it. The children of Reuben and of Gad called the altar Witness, "for it is a witness between us that the Lord is God." So, the altar remained, and all the tribes of Israel lived in peace with each other.

In closing, it is now time for Joshua to say his farewell to the leaders of Israel. He was very old and would soon die. Before his death, Joshua said to the leaders. Fear the Lord, serve Him in sincerity and in truth, and put away the gods which your fathers served on the other side of the river and in Egypt. Serve the Lord! And if it seems evil to you to serve the Lord, choose for yourselves this day whom you will serve, whether the gods of the Amorites, in whose land you dwell. But as for me and my house, we will serve the Lord."

So, the people said, "We will serve the Lord." Then Joshua said," You are a witness against yourselves that you have chosen the Lord for yourselves, to serve Him. And they said, "We are witnesses." Then Joshua wrote all their words in the book of the law. Next, he took a large stone and set it up under an oak tree that was by the sanctuary of the Lord. And Joshua said to the people, "Behold, this stone shall be a witness to us, for it has heard all the words of the Lord which He spoke to us. It shall, therefore, be a witness to you, lest you deny your God." So, Joshua let the people depart, each to his inheritance.

Here in this new phase of closing the old and ushering in the new season with the Israelites, the Lord lets us see the foreshadows of Yeshua, which is reflected through the tree that Joshua picks and the stone that was under it and calls it a witness. Yeshua was hung on a tree and is now our tree of life and our rock and is a witness to the Father so we can receive our inheritance of salvation.

Once again, God lets us see into His impeccable leadership skills through Joshua's unwavering spiritual authority and such powerful wisdom used in and throughout leading the Israelites into the promised land.

What an amazing journey Joshua had taken with all of Israel. He was 110, and it was not deterring him from completing the job that the Lord had called him to. Wow. Let us be encouraged that the Lord will always fulfill His promises if we are faithful to fill ours with Him. The words we speak are important, and they will be our witness on our behalf when we stand before the Lord one day, and that is why we, too, must choose whom we will serve this day. Amen.

Volume 3

Leadership That Restores

Chapter 1

A Sinking Boat

Have you ever been on a spiritual journey, as if you're on a boat caught in violent storms—strong winds and crashing waves threatening to overwhelm you? And despite everything, you tried to ignore the fact that it was the Lord Himself rocking the boat?

Has God called you to go and accomplish a mission for Him, and you keep refusing to do so? It is important once we have committed our life to the Lord that we learn to be obedient to His call to us. We must learn to answer quickly and respond and say, "Yes, Lord, I will go and do as you have asked me to." It is a fearful thing to fall into the hands of the Lord. However, we cannot just accept His grace and then expect just to sit back and do nothing to show Him we are grateful for what He has done for us in our lives. Having a relationship with God cannot be just one-sided. It is wise for us to do our part of serving Him without questioning all His ways when He asks us to do something that is out of our comfort zone. God will always have our best interest at heart. He will keep our way straight.

The good news is you are not alone on your journey on such matters because that is what happened to Jonah. The Lord told the prophet Jonah to go to Nineveh to share the message of repentance, or the Lord would destroy them. However, Jonah tried hard to ignore the Lord's call to go and share with the people the message of repentance. Jonah did not think that the people of Nineveh deserved God's mercy to forgive them of their great sins. He wanted God to destroy them. However, it is a good thing salvation was not Jonah's to give; it is the Lord's right to do so.

In the following chapters, we will learn more about this story, how God's saving grace happens and how using His leadership wisdom, which exemplifies His powerful negotiating skills, to bring an entire city to its knees to repent of the wickedness that had come before Him. We are never deserving of His grace, but God is willing to make an exception with those of us who have a repentant heart.

As the story goes, Jonah went down to the port of Joppa and found a ship going to Tarshish, so he paid the fare to ride on their boat and did not stay on the ship's top deck to watch the voyage out of the harbor. Instead, he went below deck, found a place to hide from the Lord and fell asleep. But the Lord sent out a great wind on the sea, and there was a mighty tempest on the sea so that the ship was about to break up. Then the mariners were afraid, and every man cried out to his god and threw the cargo that was in the ship into the sea to lighten the load.

The storm seems not to be bothering Jonah because he was fast asleep in the lowest part of the ship's belly. For he was trying to hide from the Lord; however, he forgot that you cannot hide from El Roi, the God who sees. So, the captain of the ship came to Jonah and said to him, "What do you mean, sleeper? Arise, call on your God: perhaps your God will consider us, so that we may not perish." So, the crew on the ship cast lots, and the lots fell upon Jonah. And they said to him, "Please tell us why you have caused this trouble upon us. What is your occupation? Where do you come from, and what is your country? Who are your people? So, he said to them. "I am a Hebrew, and I fear the Lord, the God of Heaven, who made the sea and the dry land." Then, the men were exceedingly afraid and decided after hearing Jonah's confession that he was running away from doing what he was told to do by the Lord, it was time to take drastic measures because the sea was becoming increasingly violent. And so finally, Jonah told the men to pick him up and throw him into the sea, and then the sea would be calm for them. Because Jonah knew he was the one who had caused this great harm to come upon the innocent men of the ship.

The men first tried to roll to shore as fast as they could, but the sea continued to become increasingly tempestuous against them. The men prayed that the Lord would not let them perish and not charge them with the innocent man's life, and so it was they picked Jonah up and threw him overboard into the sea. And immediately, the sea became calm. Can you imagine being those men and horrified by the fact that Jonah was Hebrew and a prophet of God, and now they needed to throw him into a raging sea to show God they had nothing to do with Jonah running away from Him? Wow! What would you have done in a situation like this?

Chapter 2

The Belly

Now, the Lord had prepared a great fish to swallow Jonah. It was to mirror the fact that Jonah hid from the Lord in the belly of the deepest part of the ship, and so God was granting Jonah his desire to be far away from the Lord's call to go to Nineveh, and so He put him the in the belly of a whale after Jonah was thrown into the sea. Immediately, Jonah prayed to the Lord from the belly of the fish. Let us read the prayer of Jonah from Jonah 2. It says:

> *2 I cried out to the Lord because of my affliction, and He answered me. Out of the belly of Sheol (Hell) I cried, and You heard my voice. 3 For You cast me into the deep, into the heart of the seas, and floods surrounded me; all Your billows and Your waves passed over me. 4 Then I said, 'I have been cast out of Your sight, Yet I will look again toward Your holy temple.' 5 The waters surrounded me,*

even to my soul; The deep closed around me; weeds were wrapped around my head. ⁶ I went down to the moorings of the mountains; the earth with its bars closed behind me forever; Yet you have brought up my life from the pit, O Lord, my God.

⁷ When my soul fainted within me, I remembered the Lord, and my prayer went up to You, into your holy temple.

⁸ Those who regard worthless idols forsake their own mercy. ⁹ But I will sacrifice to You with the voice of thanksgiving; I will pay what I have vowed. Salvation is of the Lord. ¹⁰ So, the Lord spoke to the fish, and it vomited Jonah onto dry land. (Jonah 2:2-10)

Oh, my goodness, can you imagine the fear of being thrown into the sea and then being swallowed by a large fish like a whale? What is amazing about this story is that Jonah had been walking by faith apparently for some time with the Lord, and his child-like faith was still intact when put into the raging sea; so much so that he first prayed to the Lord that being in the sea was deserving of his sin of disobedience. Then he reminds God that no matter where he tries to hide from Him, he will know where to find him because Jonah belonged to the Lord. Even from the deepest part of the belly of the fish, God could hear Jonah's cry for help. Therefore, Jonah, knowing this, offered a sacrifice of thanksgiving and said he would pay what he vowed to the Lord. Then Jonah admits that salvation is the Lord's to give, not his.

What tender mercies this story shows about God's leadership skills. God never stoops to harsh punishment unless it requires Him to do so. Jonah was the one who chose how the Lord was going to deal with him to fulfill his vow to the Lord. All God had to do was mirror Jonah's actions of disobedience, from the belly of the ship to the belly of the whale. God is wise and is a wise Father, and when we, His children, are acting out with unruly behavior and trying hard to do things our way, through the Father's wisdom, it will catch up with us. Outsmarting God is not a wise thing to try to do. God does not play games; it is we humans who think we can pout or fuss with God to get our way.

We should always use our words wisely when speaking to God. He judges the intent of the heart. Our own behavior or words spoken can get us in or out of trouble with the Lord. So, in the end, Jonah prayed a prayer of humility and realized he could never hide from or outsmart the Lord. Now Jonah was ready to obey the Lord and do what he was called to do with Nineveh. He then ended his prayer with thanksgiving to the Lord because he was grateful to still be alive, even though it was in the belly of a whale. Praise broke the chain of bondage. God showed Jonah just how important salvation is by placing him in a dark place away from the presence of the Lord so he would know what would happen to the people of Nineveh if they should perish without the Lord's salvation.

Life and death are in the tongue, and Jonah was now ready to be obedient and speak life to the very people he did not think deserved God's grace because of their great sin against the Lord. We are to remember God's plan is salvation for all men. Thank God for the tender mercies He showed to Jonah and the people of Nineveh, or we might not have had the opportunity to experience His love and mercy on the day of our salvation. I am truly thankful to the Lord for saving me.

Bless the Lord and all that is within me, for He is greatly to be praised!

Chapter 3

Another Opportunity

Now that God had Jonah's full attention by letting the fish spit Jonah up on the seashore, He would give Jonah another opportunity to set things right with Him:

> *¹ The Word came to Jonah the second time, saying, ² 'Arise, go to Nineveh, that great city, and preach to it the message that I tell you.' ³ So Jonah arose and went to Nineveh, according to the Word of the Lord. Now, Nineveh was an exceedingly great city, a three-day journey in extent. ⁴ And Jonah began to enter the city on the first day's walk. Then he cried out and said, 'Yet forty days, and Nineveh shall be overthrown!'*

Sometimes, when God speaks to you and tells you to speak out and proclaim a message to a person or people, do not be slow to respond and react to do it. We must move fast, especially when you know without any doubt that the Lord has called upon you to share a message that will change the course of the wicked to righteousness. Jonah knew he would feel out of place and sounded like a lunatic shouting out that in forty days, Nineveh would be overthrown. It did not matter how silly he looked or sounded because it was God speaking through him to change the evil hearts of the people to repent before they were destroyed.

The amazing thing was that God's Spirit was traveling with Jonah, already making his way straight so that the people would receive the message and turn from their wicked ways. The people took the message being spoken of by Jonah so seriously that it reached the King of Nineveh, and he commanded all the people and all animals to wear sackcloth and to fast from food or drink. All the people were to cry out mightily to God and turn from their evil ways and from the violence that was in their hands.

> *⁹ Who can tell if God will turn and relent, and turn away His fierce anger, so that we may not perish?*
>
> *¹⁰ Then God saw the works, that they turned from their evil way; and God relented from the disaster that He had said He would bring upon them, and He did not do it. (Jonah 3:9-10)*

How powerful! See how important it is to get out of our comfort zone when God calls upon us to share the message of repentance with whomever He has told us to. Our ways are not the Lord's, obviously, and probably for a good reason since we tend to be slow to do what the Lord has told us to. I do not know about you, but I am learning through this message about Jonah that I should be quick to respond when God calls me to "go and do" a mission for Him.

Another interesting thing about Jonah is that he was one of the first missionaries that God commissioned to go out to a people that were not His to share the good news of the Lord's mercy.

In Matthew 12:39-41, it says that some of the scribes and Pharisees told Jesus that they wanted to see a sign from Him.

> [39] But He answered and said to them: 'An evil and adulterous generation seeks after a sign, and no sign will be given to it except the sign of the prophet Jonah. [40] For as Jonah was three days and three nights in the belly of the great fish, so will the Son of Man be three days and three nights in the heart of the earth. [41] The men of Nineveh will rise in the judgment with this generation and condemn it because they repented at the preaching of Jonah, and indeed, greater than Jonah is here.'

The story of Jonah was a foreshadow of Jesus the Messiah and that God moved in place at that time because He knew what needed to be done to set salvation in motion for all mankind. Jonah was like a messiah in that day and time for he was born for such a time to bring the good news of God's love and mercy to a lost generation of gentile people. Amen.

Chapter 4

Kindness

And so it was that Jonah preached the good news of repentance to the people of Nineveh for three days and then went and camped on the east side of the outer city limits so that he could sit and watch Nineveh be destroyed. When God did not destroy Nineveh because they repented and changed their evil ways, Jonah became angry at God. He desired to see them destroyed because they were wicked and they were Gentiles. Hebrews were not allowed to associate with Gentiles in those days. However, Jonah had forgotten that God had shown him mercy while in the belly of the great fish and that God is the Creator of all mankind.

Jonah explained to God that he had fled his homeland to escape His presence because he knew that God was gracious and merciful—slow to anger and abundant in lovingkindness, relenting from disaster. Jonah then asked God to take his life, feeling bitter about the mercy shown to Nineveh.

Then the Lord said, 'Is it right for you to be angry?' (Jonah 4:4)

Despite this, Jonah sat outside the city, having built a shelter, still hoping to see Nineveh's destruction. Meanwhile, the Lord showed kindness to Jonah and had a huge plant that grew up over his shelter to give him shade, and Jonah was grateful for the plant. But as morning dawned the next day, God prepared a worm, and it damaged the plant so much that it withered.

And it happened, when the sun arose, that God prepared a forceful east wind, and the sun beat on Jonah's head so that he grew faint. Then, once again, he wanted to die and said, "It is better for me to die than to live."

⁹ Then God said to Jonah, 'Is it right for you to be angry about the plant?'

And he said, 'It is right for me to be angry, even to death!'

¹⁰ But the Lord said: 'You have had pity on the plant which you have not labored, nor made it grow, which came up in a night and perished in a night. ¹¹ And should I not pity Nineveh, that great city, in which there are more than one hundred and twenty thousand persons who cannot discern between their right hand and their left and much livestock?' (Jonah 4:9-10)

So, the moral of this story could be of two things: God knew that Jonah needed a change of heart of wanting the wicked not to be saved, so that is why He chose Jonah for the job. And second, you should not want bad things to happen to wicked people just because you think they deserve it.

Matthew 9:10-13 tells the story of Jesus and the disciples sitting down at a table, and many sinners and tax collectors came and sat down with them:

> *¹¹ And when the Pharisees saw it, they said to His disciples, 'Why does your teacher eat with the tax collectors and sinners?'*
>
> *¹² When Jesus heard that, He said to them: 'Those who are well have no need of a physician, but those who are sick. ¹³ But go and learn what this means: I desire mercy and not sacrifice, for I did not come to call the righteous, but sinners, to repentance.'*

This is another wow moment; here, Jonah's story was truly reflecting Jesus' ministry to come. And it was bearing witness to the one and true power that only God Himself is a merciful leader and can give unadulterated love and forgiveness with sincere kindness to a wicked generation, casting off the hardness of a sinful heart to draw near to the Lord.

Let us fall to our knees today in prayer to pray for our relatives, friends, and strangers in our cities. Forgive us, Lord, for having selfish ambitions and not being careful to stop and pray for those who are lost without you. I thank you for your kindness towards me and all those who You have called according to your purpose.

Yes, Lord! My soul thirsts for you; bless the Lord and all that is within me; bless His holy name. Amen.

Chapter 5

Rebuild

Sometimes, there are areas in our lives that may have become shambles while we become compliant and lazy. We lost our focus on what was important. However, with the Lord, it is never too late for a second chance. Sometimes, all we need is the right encouragement from an extraordinary leader who understands the principle of the concept of the word "rebuild." And so, it was for Nehemiah, who was a true man of God; he had a heart for Jerusalem and the people of Israel. He was living in exile and was a cupbearer for a Persian king.

Nehemiah had heard about Jerusalem being in shambles and wept bitterly before the Lord. He prayed and was fasting for many days, seeking instructions from the Lord on what to do. He was not a man of complaining or making excuses for why the city of Jerusalem was sitting in disrepair. And so it was Nehemiah prayed to the Lord God of Heaven:

⁵ O great and awesome God, You who keep your covenant and mercy with those who love You and observe Your commandments, ⁶ please let Your ear be attentive and Your eyes open, that You may hear the prayer of Your servant which I pray before You now, day and night, for the children of Israel Your servants, and confess the sins of the children of Israel which we have sinned against You. Both my father's house and I have sinned.

⁷ We have acted very corruptly against You and have not kept the commandments, the statutes, nor the ordinances which You commanded Your servant, Moses. ⁸ Remember, I pray, the word that You commanded Your servant Moses, saying, 'If you are not faithful, I will scatter you among the nations; ⁹ but if you return to Me, and keep My commandments and do them, though some of you were cast out to the farthest part of the heavens, yet I will gather them from there and bring them to the place which I have chosen as a dwelling for My name.' ¹⁰ Now these are Your servants and Your people, whom You have redeemed by Your great power and by Your strong hand. ¹¹ O Lord, I pray, please let Your ear be attentive to the prayer of Your servant, and to the prayer of Your servants who desire to fear Your name; and let Your servant prosper this day; I pray and grant him mercy in the sight of this man." For I was the King's cupbearer.

It is important for us to understand the prayer that Nehemiah prayed because there are times that we need to own up to the sin that has been committed because sometimes you and your forefathers committed the sin that caused the shambles in your life to happen. He was repenting of his sin of breaking the covenant to follow the commandments the Israelites had vowed before the Lord with Moses. And now he was willing to lay down his life for the purpose of making a new commitment to serve the Lord by getting God's permission to rebuild Jerusalem walls where needed for the safety and spiritual nutriment of his people Israel.

I do not know about you, but Nehemiah's prayer is extremely sincere, powerful and heart-touching. It is wise for us to speak plainly to the Lord when we are praying for a move on His behalf. Our prayers can move mountains, cause the sun and moon to stop, whatever we need, we can make a petition to the Lord, and because He judges us by the intent of our heart, He will answer and give us the wisdom to know how to rebuild the holes in the walls that have appeared in our lives that have kept out the enemy in past times.

And now, here in Persia, as the king's cupbearer, the Spirit of God was calling a man named Nehemiah to step out of his comfort zone and return to Jerusalem and gather His people to rebuild its damaged walls. No doubt, the task of rebuilding those gaps in the walls was going to be difficult but would be rewarding in the end. And so it was; God let Nehemiah win favor with the King and

Queen, and they allowed him to go to Jerusalem to help His people rebuild the broken walls. The King also gave him papers that gave him permission to pass from one region to the next while traveling to Judah. And he was able to gather the necessary supplies and wood to accomplish the mission the Lord had called him too for the rebuild. Once again, we can learn that when the Lord has commissioned us to do something, we can know that if it is His will, it is His bill. You will lack nothing for the journey for the task at hand. Amen.

Chapter 6

In the Night

Nehemiah's story just keeps getting better and better. After arriving in Jerusalem, he was there for three days. Then he arose in the night, he, and a few men with him; he told no one what God had put in his heart to do at Jerusalem. He and the men survey the walls during the night so as not to draw attention to what he was planning. He told the men,

> *'You see the distress that we are in, how Jerusalem lies waste, and its gates are burned with fire. Come let us build the wall of Jerusalem, that we may no longer be a reproach.' (Nehemiah 2:17)*

Next, he told the men with him of the hand of God, which had been good upon him, and of the King's word that he had spoken to him:

> *So they said, 'Let us rise up and build,' Then they set their hands to this good work. (Nehemiah 2:18)*

Sometimes, it is good to be quiet about what the Lord is planning through your ministry so the enemy or those who just love to cause negative talk against you, so as to deter you from accomplishing what God has called you to do so it will arouse others to help them to stop you from completing the task you have been assigned to by the Lord. Nehemiah was using wisdom to move around in the night quietly to decide the best way to bring about rebuilding the holes in the wall of Jerusalem. By doing so, he was able to begin with a few men catching the vision to rebuild the walls and gates of God's beloved city.

Now just what Nehemiah suspected would happen after he and the men started on the project of the rebuild manifested. There came three men who laughed at them and said:

> [19] 'What is this thing you are doing? Will you rebel against the King?' [20] So I answered them, and said to them. 'The God of Heaven Himself will prosper us; therefore, we, His servants, will arise and build, but you have no heritage or right or memorial in Jerusalem.' (Nehemiah 2:19-20)

Oh, my goodness, it was like he was saying to them what Jesus said when He was being tempted in the wilderness, "Get behind Me, Satan! For it is written, you shall worship the Lord your God, and Him only you shall serve."[5]

------

[5] Luke 4:8

Wow! Nehemiah stepped up to the plate and hit a home run here for sure. He boldly stood up for the work of the Lord and flat-out told those guys they had no heritage in what they were doing. Absolutely, troublemakers do not have a heritage with us that are called to do the work of the Lord. Nehemiah was staying focused and was not going to let the negative men stop them. He was on a mission for God, and so everyone who was against them just needed to step out of the way.

But it so happened when the man, Sanballat, heard that they were building the wall, that he was furious and terribly angry and mocked the Jews. He gathered others against them. Then Nehemiah prayed a prayer that the Lord would stop the enemy and cause the enemy's own destruction to fall back on their own heads.

The men continued to work building the walls and fixing the gates to the city even though they would get attacked by those who did not want the Jews to succeed in finishing the job. So, Nehemiah produced a plan for the men to keep working by stationing every family near the job sites, and he gave them (and the men hiding below the wall) spears, swords and bows to protect them while they worked. He taught them to work with a spear in their hand while they rebuilt the walls.

This story gives us a symbolic picture of how important it is to stand in the gap spiritually for family and friends in times of need and salvation. Prayer is a powerful tool to stop the enemy from breaching the walls of protection around us. Let us put on the full armor of God so that we can stand in the days of evil. And so it happened, when their enemies heard that it was known to the workers, and that God had brought their plot to nothing, that all of them returned to the wall, everyone to his work. So it was, from that time on, that half of the men worked at construction, while the other half held the spears, the shields, the bow, and wore armor, and the leaders were behind the house of Judah. Now, they were driven to finish. Nehemiah told the people, "Do not be afraid of them. Remember the Lord, great and awesome, and fight for your brethren, your sons, your daughters, your wives, and your houses" (Nehemiah 4:14). For they knew that God would fight for them; there was no turning back.

Chapter 7

A New Mind Set

The walls of Jerusalem were finished; the people had persevered and overcome the entire negative from the region's locals. Now, they had a new mindset to continue forward and see what else the Lord had in store for their new beginnings in Jerusalem. In chapter 5, Nehemiah has become the governor of Jerusalem, the land of Judah. He called a meeting for all the people to come too. Eventually, he found out just how oppressed they were. He listened to their stories, and most of the Jews were extremely in debt and had borrowed money to pay their taxes. They had to sell some of their daughters into slavery and could not afford to get them back because other men owned their land and vineyards.

And so it was, Nehemiah talked to all the Jews and explained how they should have forgiven their brethren of all their debt after seven years as it was written in the law to do so. And so, it was all the brethren who forgave one another's debt, and it was restored, and the community of the people was forgiven. Next, Nehemiah called the priests and required an oath from them that they would do according to the promise. And all the assembly agreed and did according to the promise.

Nehemiah's generosity, as the people's new governor, decided not to ever take any food, drink or money from the people because all the leaders before him mistreated the people and took advantage of them by putting them in bondage. Therefore, he chooses to be kind and not take from their provisions. Most definitely Nehemiah was reflecting God's leadership by showing unconditional love and concern for the people. He desired to see them prosper and not live in oppression. God does desire to see His own live in prosperity.

Once again, the enemies of the Jews tried extremely hard to trick Nehemiah into meeting with them secretly so they could harm his good name to the King. However, he was not fooled by the deception of evildoers. Nehemiah was grounded in the Lord's trust and, therefore, continued straight ahead with his plans to grow a new mindset in all the Jews that had helped rebuild the city walls.

Have you ever had others try to scare you out of the blessings of the Lord? Satan is a liar and comes to kill, steal and destroy, and that is what he was trying to do with Nehemiah by using evil people who were jealous and envious of the good works of the people. They were not going to be able to keep oppressing the Jews and stealing from them anymore. Like Nehemiah, we must stand our ground when we know 100% that God has called us to complete His work. Stay the course and do not look to left or right, looking straight ahead, we will win the battle. For the battle belongs to the Lord.

And so it was, Nehemiah reformed the people by having Ezra read the book of the Law of Moses to them (chapter 8), and they began to cry upon hearing the laws, for it had been a long time since they had heard the book of the laws. Ezra told the people, "Do not sorrow, for the joy of the Lord is your strength." I do not know about you, but about right now, I feel the Spirit of the Lord, tug at my heart. There have been dry seasons in my spiritual walk with the Lord, and I went for several months without picking up His Word and reading it. My heart is saddened by that, and I fully understand what those people must have been feeling when Ezra read the Book of Laws to them.

It was the feast of Tabernacles after the walls were finished, and the people were told to go out and prepare to build their Sukkoth booths. They assembled for seven days, and then on the twenty-fourth day, they fasted in sackcloth with dust on their heads. And then those of the Israelite lineage separated themselves from all foreigners, and they stood and confessed their sins and the iniquities of their fathers. How powerful; they were coming full circle back to the original plan God had set in place for them.

Somehow, they got off track and fell away from the Lord and His ways; I am so glad God believes in second chances.

The Israelites were sealing the covenant again with the Lord and were now ready for a new, fresh start and prepared to live for the Lord once again and not compromise truth for false ways. God is an amazing, gentle leader and shows kindness towards us who have fallen away by allowing us to repent and renew our vow to serve Him all the days of our lives. We must seek first His kingdom and righteousness, and He will set things right for us to prosper once again, making our way straight.

Chapter 8

A Leader

Nehemiah had his work cut out for him. As a leader for God, he had to bring the Israelites back to their first love of serving the Lord. Once he had observed and figured out the cause of the oppression among his people, he was able to start teaching the old paths like Jeremiah teaches us to do so. Sometimes, new ways are not the perfect way to follow, especially if God has set forth a particular direction; He has called you to observe and live by what is good for you.

Being a leader in the ministry for the Lord has its challenges because you will always need to keep yourself in check and accountable to God and a community of other leaders as well. Satan loves rogue leaders because that is where he can fool them into thinking they have all the answers, and everyone must worship their way of leadership because they are in authority. However, Nehemiah's style of leadership was based on the Lord's care for His people. Truly, God does not want to take advantage of us but wants us to learn to set boundaries in our lives that set the pace to live a righteous life before Him.

God requires us to live by His statutes and His righteousness that does not mirror the secular world. When we as believers mirror the secular world, we forget the old paths, the good ways of the Lord.

Jeremiah 6:16 says:

Stand in the ways and see, and ask for the old paths, where the good way is, and walk in it; then you will find rest for your souls.

This is what Nehemiah was out to accomplish: to bring his people back to their former ways because they had forgotten them, and it would bring back the much-needed rest they were missing in their lives.

As a leader, there was no glamour in it for Nehemiah; he was on a mission for the Lord and was not going to detour from it. Notice how Nehemiah got the Israelites on board to go back to their first love of serving the Lord. He began with a small group of men from among the tribes and took them out in the quiet of the night on a secret mission for God to survey the city walls of Jerusalem. And once the men saw what God was calling Nehemiah to do for their people it was easier to get them on board to accomplish the move of God restoring and rebuilding the walls of the city. From then on Nehemiah continued to meet the needs of the people and lead them into overcoming their past failures of allowing their city and their lives that had become full of shame among the heathen nations that were living among them.

Now, the children of Israel could not even be recognized by the style of life they were living among the foreigners. They had totally gotten away from the covenant they had made on Mount Sinai and when they had crossed over the river Jordan with Joshua. They were marrying the foreigners, worshiping their pagan gods and were in debt to them.

Nehemiah had to separate the tribes again, cleanse the children of Israel from pagan practices, and purify their style of living before the Lord. Now, there were some tribes that had mixed among the pagans with marriage and so forth, and they had to be removed from among those who had not violated the Lord's statutes on these matters.

Once Nehemiah had chosen who would live inside the gates of Jerusalem by setting back the order the Lord had required of the children of Israel, he was able to start closing the gates of the city on the day of Sabbath. There was to be no selling, working, or trading on this seventh day of the week, which was a Saturday. God wanted them to rest one day a week from all their burdens because, eventually, that is what got them into the bad habit of the pagans and backsliding, not observing God's commandments they had agreed to long ago.

So, a good question for a believer in Jesus is, do you practice the old ways that lead to the good ways of the Lord? Can God distinguish who you are among the secular world? Let us bring all our ways and thoughts into the captivity of the mind of our savior, Jesus. Let our hearts reflect our outer person for the Lord that sets us apart from the world. I do not know about you, but when the roll is called up yonder, I want to be included to live within God's city gates in the Kingdom He created for us to enjoy living in His presence and peace for all eternity. Amen.

Chapter 9

Restoration

God always has a thoughtful plan through His gracious leadership, yet it may seem stern and frightening at times, but it is not. God is so gracious when it comes to the restoration of His children and the sins they have committed. Like any good Father, God will show grace before having to correct our crooked way. Has your earthly dad ever said to you, "if you do not get your act together, I am going to send you to your room or take your cell phone or car keys away" and so forth? Well, that shows you grace before handing out the punishment for the disobedience you really deserve, before the hammer falls. When dad or mom must step in and say enough is enough, it is because it is true, and most likely, they will say," I gave you a warning to correct the error of your way, and it is time to pay the pied piper." Eventually sin catches up with us and the consequences that come with it as well.

I do not know about you, but I would rather heed God's grace to change my ways immediately before His grace ran out, and I had to pay the price for my disobedience. God is about bringing restoration to our lives. He loves to see His children live in peace and prosper in all their ways.

I love the story of Jeremiah because he was called as a young man by God to be a prophet. His main ministry was to bring restoration to the Hebrews. Judah was being called out for her sins against God. It is interesting that God spoke to them through Jeremiah like a father would with any child of his that had gone astray.

Jeremiah 2:2-3 says:

2 Go and cry in the hearing of Jerusalem, saying, 'Thus says the Lord: "I remember you, the kindness of your youth, and the love of your betrothal. When you went after Me in the wilderness, in a land not sown, 3 Israel was holiness to the Lord, the first fruits of His increase; all that devour him will offend; Disaster will come upon them," says the Lord.'

Then, in verse four, the Lord asks them, *"What injustice have your fathers found in Me?"*

The point the Lord was driving at was that He had brought them into the Land of milk and honey, and they forgot the promise they had made to Him to follow His ways that were set up to give them peace, structure, and values to live by. Yet here they were again, falling away from faithfulness to their heavenly Father.

Over and over, He guided them and gave them prosperity because of their obedience and the love they had for Him in the times past. So, like Judah, why is it that we, as His children, cannot stay the course? He has called us once we think He is not looking at or paying attention to what we are doing in our lives.

God will never bring judgment upon us for the sheer fun of it. It is not His way. He is gracious to us and tries to first get us to see the error of our ways. What a good Father He is.

Jeremiah 2:13 says:

For my peoples have committed evils; they have forsaken Me, the fountain of living waters, and hewn themselves cisterns-broken cisterns that can hold no water.

Wow, what that means is when we are a broken spirit inwardly, how can we hold the full living waters of our God that gives us life? A life that is full of His care and grace, a life that gives us the blessing of salvation. A life that gives corrections because He loves us enough to bring the opportunity of restoration to us when we have fallen into sin; what an amazing God that He is, so much so that He wants us not to be broken but to live a life full of His Holy Spirit that the only way it will flow out of our spiritual water jar is because it overflows from the top from all the blessings He has bestowed upon us and not out the broken cracks from our sins. What a great picture that scripture paints of Jesus, who is our Living Water; He was bruised for our transgressions and became that broken vessel so we could have salvation and live life whole and not broken.

God told Jeremiah to tell the people He would give them shepherds according to His heart, who would feed them with knowledge and understanding. Thank God, Jesus was willing to be the head shepherd who became a leader who taught twelve men to follow in His footsteps so broken mankind could learn of His salvation and experience restoration for all generations to come. Powerful indeed!

Chapter 10

Spoken Hope

Jeremiah's prophesy to Israel is about a spoken hope that would be in the near and distance future. Composing the spoken Word of hope from the Lord to them is like piecing a large puzzle together with many different tiny components that will eventually connect to each other to make a complete picture of what their present and future will look like for them.

There were many diverse types of ways to convey the spoken hope that the Lord was releasing upon Israel. It would not be without the consequences of the sins they had committed. The Lord was faithful to keep all His promises to the children of Israel and yet somehow, they could not find it in them to stay the course to live in the secured hope of the Lord. And it is the same with modern men; we, too, find it hard to live in that same secure hope.

We can rejoice that the Lord is always far ahead of us, making His spoken hope with some second-chance adjustments that are powered by His loving leadership that reflects His grace, regardless of the intent of our sinful hearts. In another aspect of Jeremiah's prophecy, we are told to observe the potter and learn that we cannot decide to be shaped how we want but that we will be used for the purpose we were formed too, which means we were formed as humans, male or female and no matter how you try to think outside of that perspective you can never be anything less than that. So, we must learn to rejoice in the hope that the potter's vision for His creation is meant for good and not harm, as He told Jeremiah in chapter 29:10-14.

God created us in His image. He molded us to perform in the same like manner He does and that is why we must learn respect, for He cares for us. We were not created by chance. He is showing us we were intentionally made by telling Jeremiah in chapter 1, verse 5 that He knew him before He formed him in the womb. Before he was born, the Lord sanctified him to be a prophet to the nations. This is amazing because evil men in this age would have you think that is not true. They would have you think they have control of human life and can re-create a human into something God did not plan from the beginning of time. We must be the ones to say that enough is enough; I will follow the plans of the Lord for my life. If you do not know what that plan is, then you have not been reading His Word on a regular basis to find out. The Israelites kept falling away because they stopped meeting together and reading the plans the Lord had for them through His living

Word. We are created for fellowship with our Maker, and He desires to see us not live in fear but in peace.

I would imagine being Jeremiah was no walk in the park. God had assigned him a task that would call for him to be arrested and put in a dungeon full of wet, dirty mud, and the only way out of it was to pull him up from above where the door was. It sounds to me like it was no glamour job. Has God called you to ministry? If so, be prepared to get your hands dirty. Not all work for the Lord is going to be as easy or glamorous as some would have you think. Sometimes, He may call you to deliver a message like Jeremiah, who knows, but as He told him:

Do not be afraid; I will be with you.

The Lord spoke to Jeremiah while he was in prison and said to purchase his cousin's land outside of the Jerusalem walls, even though the enemy had their soldiers living on the property. So that after the 70-year captivity was over he would be able to still claim land for his family. This was another step of faith for Jeremiah to trust the Lord to bring about the future for his family, which would bear hope in them to have a place to go back to after captivity.

Jeremiah was told to tell the Israelites that they would be cast into exile in captivity for 70 years because of their sins of disobedience. They had broken all the statues of the Lord. However, even while handing out their punishment the Lord had spoken hope for them as well. He told them after 70 years, He would bring them back from captivity from all over the world, and once again, He would put His spirit in them, and they would again have a heart for God and desire to know and live in His care once and for all. It says in Jeremiah 31 that He will replenish their weary souls and bless them, and it goes on to say that everyone shall die for his own iniquity:

> [31] 'Behold the days are coming, says the Lord, when I will make a new covenant with the house of Israel and with the house of Judah—[32] not according to the covenant that I made with their fathers in that day that I took them by the hand to lead them out of the land of Egypt, My covenant which they broke, though I was a husband to them, says the Lord. [33] But this is the covenant that I will make with the house of Israel after those days, says the Lord: I will put My law in their minds, and write it on their hearts; and I will be their God, and they shall be My people. [34] No more shall every man teach his neighbor, and every man his brother, saying, "Know the Lord," for they all shall know Me, from the least of them to the greatest of them, says the Lord. For I will forgive their iniquity, and their sin I will remember no more.'

What a great picture of His spoken hope for their future because it has ended up the Gentiles' future of hope as well. Jeremiah's prophecy was a pure picture of Yeshua, the Messiah coming and would be the spoken law, the spoken Word written on our minds and hearts for all time, from sea to shining sea, from coast to coast across the world.

The covenant of Redemption was made new for future generations among the nations around the world because now God would hold each individual person responsible for their own sins. The Lamb of God would be that new covenant once and for all, and now we would be allowed back into the New Jerusalem, which God Himself will send out a surveyor to plumb straight lines so He Himself will build a new city where Nehemiah and Ezra had rebuilt the walls of Jerusalem 200 years before Jeremiah came along and prophesied this new covenant.

The Lord says in Jeremiah 33:

15 In those days and at that time I will cause to grow up to David a Branch of righteousness; he shall execute judgment and righteousness in the earth. 16 In those days Judah will be saved, and Jerusalem will dwell safely. And this is the name by which she will be called: THE Lord OUR RIGHTEOUSNESS. (Jeremiah 33:15-16)

Wow! Judah will have a new name, erasing her past sins.

Jeremiah is a great book for the Lord to use to complete this book. How powerfully the Lord is willing to gently guide us through lessons on His leadership so we can better understand why He leads the way He does from the beginning of time to the return of the Messiah. His ways are not our ways, and His thoughts are not ours, for I AM is a God who leads.

Description

*I*AM: *The God Who Leads* is a transformative journey through 30 captivating short stories, divided into three volumes. Each volume, containing 10 chapters, delves into God's divine leadership and invites readers to explore His wisdom in leading His people. Through thought-provoking narratives, this book offers fresh perspectives on God's leadership as revealed in Scripture, showcasing the various ways He guides His people toward success, fulfillment, and purpose.

Each story challenges readers to view leadership through God's eyes, encouraging a deeper understanding of His methods, wisdom, and intentional guidance. As the stories unfold, readers will gain valuable insights into how God's leadership can impact not only their personal faith but also their roles in families, churches, workplaces, and communities.

This book aims to inspire readers to embrace God's leadership in their own lives, sharpening their own leadership skills with divine wisdom that can bring favor in all areas of life. Whether you are seeking to grow spiritually or lead more effectively in your daily life, *I AM: The God Who Leads* will leave you with a newfound hunger to learn more about God's powerful, intentional, and sovereign leadership.

About the Author

V alerie Henderson is an American author who loves writing short stories that are inspirational and spiritually uplifting to encourage others to live righteously before the Lord while growing and maturing in His care. Valerie has been a guest speaker on radio shows, in churches, Bible studies, events and podcasts.

Valerie is the author of *November 8th*, *The Read Me Color Book, Grace to Run the Race*, and *The Keys to the Kingdom of Heaven.*

Published by:

Scroll

PUBLISHERS

A division of LifeSpring Publishing

www.scrollpublishers.com

Has God spoken to you about writing a book?
Let us help you!

www.ingramcontent.com/pod-product-compliance
Lightning Source LLC
Chambersburg PA
CBHW020900090426
42736CB00008B/439